mama, bare

volume 1, the birth of mother

we have written this
for all mothers.
dedicated to laura & iris.

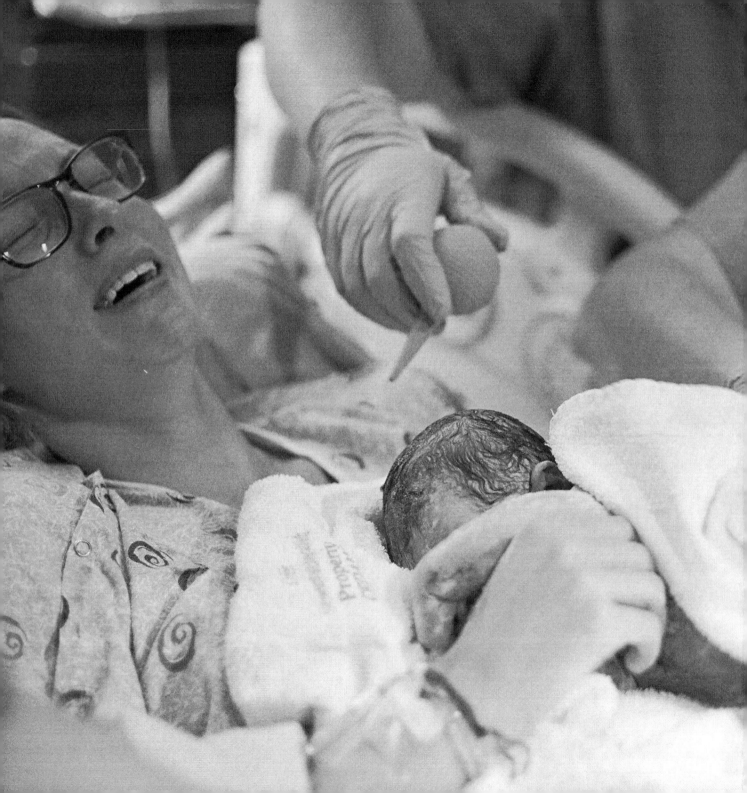

I [...] striking to me. Even now, eight months after her birth, I study it as if there's something I've missed. I count the details, nodding. Sticky white skin, hands opening and closing like someone kneading bread, the smell of iron and sweat and the salt of the sea. In this moment, I was feeling the most profound and painful love that a person can feel. And in that same moment, a half of me was dying. The selfish half. The running half. The half that always flies away when things get difficult. I was born then, too, in that moment. Trembling, exploding from old skin and growing fast into something strange, and smoldering, and beautiful.

I woke quickly on the morning of the third day of Aspen's earthen life and knew that I was wildly different. I sat up in the sheets and felt as if I weighed nothing at all. Half a person, I thought. I was constructed of bones balanced on bones, paper thin skin, a still swollen womb. The emptiness was countered by love, of course, by joy, by the sweet smelling skin of a peachy new babe. Over the following first months of her life, I had room within my bones for Mother to swell, to fill all the empty spaces, to grow new skin over old bruises and become the woman I was created to be. But it was difficult. Possibly even more difficult than the act of giving birth.

Stories of birth are celebrated and shared freely, as they should be. But the hollow moments afterward - the first day, the first week, the first month - are a strange and foreign place to be, and are hardly talked about at all. In my opinion, this leaves new mothers feeling forced to carry on as if nothing much has changed. They stumble into motherhood blindly, uncomfortable in new skin, fumbling with the wanting body of a newborn, and the birth of a Mother, and the death of an Ego.

This book is a collection of fleeting moments. Moments of birth, of death, of swelling spirits and overflowing joy. Moments that turn our hearts to honey. Moments that shatter us. That stitch us back together, stronger, wiser, more beautiful. That illuminate the path to healing. The moments when we became Mother. More than anything, my hope is that you hold this book in your palms and feel that it is holding you, too.

breathe slowly, dear one.

these stories
are for you.

I'm learning
to make space
for the pieces
of the girl
I was.

There was a time, a long time, before you, when I belonged entirely to myself. Sometimes I sit and remember that girl - the careless way she traveled through the world, the ease with which she made plans and changed them, her fearless daring heart that jumped and risked and broke and stacked up sleepless nights like they were nothing but fuel for her mischievous fire. Some days I miss her terribly, miss her like a limb or a purpose or home. Some days I envy her freedom and her callousness and her vanity. Some days I sit for long minutes and simply wonder where on earth she has gone.

You are the sort of thing that bends time, my beautiful, precious you.

Even as I remember the girl who was before you, I can't wrap my heart around a time when you weren't with me, as though you were something always carried, somewhere in my girlhood and my singleness and our early marriage, something always waiting to come and break and mend everything all at once. I remember the velvet, other-worldly softness of your newborn body, your wide open eyes that came firm with the knowing that now there would be only after you, that from now on everything I am would be tied to the simple truth that you are.

You are.

You are, and because you are, I will be something other than the girl I was. My fate, from the moment of your birth and with all of my heart, is tied to the fact of you. It's a beautiful truth - one that heals, and bends, and breaks, and challenges, one that I have raged against and clung to and been grateful for with a depth I couldn't imagine before you. You are, and because you are, I am altered. You are, and because you are, I am yours.

I am learning to make space for the pieces of the girl that I was. I am learning to introduce her to you, to our life here, to let you grab onto her ambitions and her selfishness and her gorgeous careless soul with your perfect little fingers that leave your perfectly indelible mark. Because it's us from here on out - because the girl I was and the girl I am because of you and your sweet smile are the puzzle pieces that make up your mother, and we, all of

6

us, belong to each other.

I will give you all of her stories, all of mine, and we will write ours. I will give you the most beautiful things that I know, I will love you with all the ferocity I can muster, and I will be your mother. I have been her all along.

She wakes before I do, with the slow moving journey of the sun, and I feel her eyes before I see them. her little hands are opening and closing like oysters, like she's grabbing at subtle things that I cannot see, like she's listening to the sound of her baby bones creaking. The room is cold and fresh with the flavor of morning. for a moment I can smell what my house smells like to strangers. Vanilla honey. Old laundry. Oak and pine and damp earth. I smile, watching.

"How are things going?"

I always respond that things are going great, that I'm so happy, and make myself seem so strong, but now, I'm going to be honest. I'm weak, I'm breaking, I'm trembling, I'm losing it. I've always made this single mother thing seem like the best thing, but I fucking hate it.

It's hurts so bad, loving this little guy so much, and knowing what he's going to face. Having to try and be strong for the both of us when I barely am strong enough for myself, looking at his little face, in his little eyes and knowing one day, that little soul of his might lose itself through the sadness. I can't do it. I hate this. I hate being a single mother. I hate it so much.

It's 2:33 a.m. and I can barely breathe.
It's 2:33 a.m. and I can barely see.

I don't know how I'm doing as a mother. I mean, people say I'm doing a good job, but sometimes I feel like I have no idea what I'm doing. That I'm failing. It's two in the morning, and Dakota is screaming his head off, he won't stop, I won't stop. People say being a mother is so hard, and no, it isn't. It's easy to be a mother. It's easy to nurture the little soul. It's easy to teach them, to watch them grow, to snuggle them to make them feel safe. It's hard to be the mother and father. It's hard to be your own support system at two in the morning where you're at the point where you say you don't want to live. It's hard to keep yourself and the baby happy, healthy. It's hard to keep going when everything is facing down.

But it's 2:42, and it's easy. It's easy to love the little guy, to give him a bottle and see his hand touching your hand, your chest, your cheek. To see his eyes full of tears, but still smiling. It's easy to know that you're being both parents, and he's healthy, he's going to be somebody big, somebody wonderful. It's easy to live, because this little guy is going to need you, going to want you, going to grow with you.

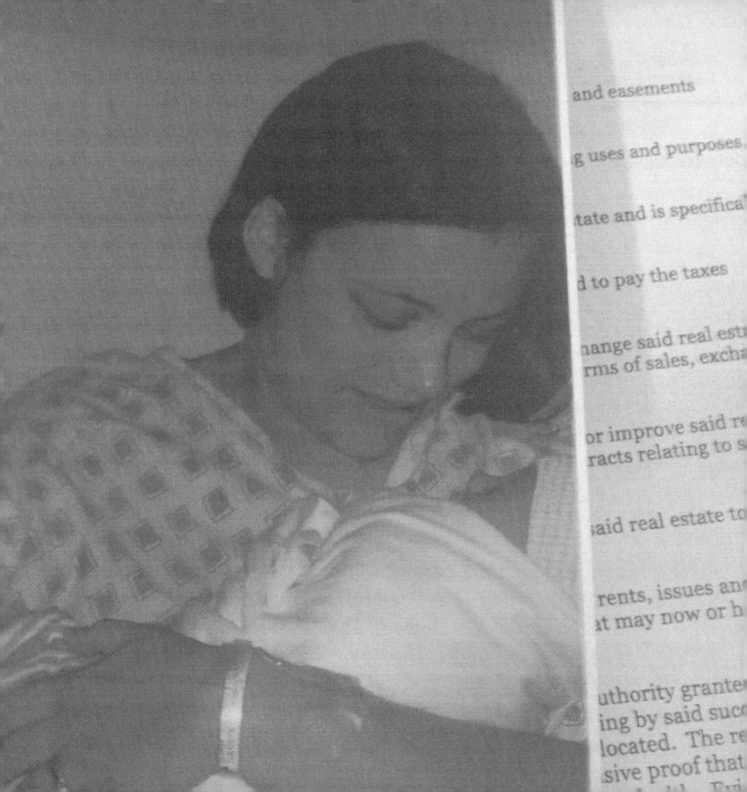

and easements

g uses and purposes,

tate and is specifica

d to pay the taxes

hange said real est
rms of sales, excha

or improve said re
racts relating to s

said real estate to

rents, issues an
at may now or h

uthority grante
ing by said suc
located. The re
sive proof that

As soon as I saw his face, as soon as they placed him on my now empty womb, I became someone else. In that very moment, I was transformed, evolved, reborn. His birth and my rebirth happened simultaneously, and only because I carried him did I get to carry myself. Nurture myself, grow my own roots into the garden of motherhood where I still remain.

Henry wasn't planned. In fact, upon finding out there was a life growing inside me, more than anything I felt like a loss had happened. I grieved my old life, not yet knowing what loss I was grieving other than the death of my selfishness. I knew that much: motherhood equaled the dying of self. It wasn't until he was earth side that I realized what else had died that day.

That first month, it was as if I was living in a dream state. Oxytocin flowed freely and I sat suspended between euphoria and the reality of our new little nest. Our new little family. I was so fragile, tentative, felt as if I was dancing on broken glass and the slightest jerky movement would split the soles of my feet wide open. That was what it felt like that first month. Like I was being broken open over and over. And every time I did, I bled a little more of my old self into the abyss. A little more of my old self was drained out and a new, more soulful, gentle human being took my place.

See, that first month? I was grieving the illusion that life was about choosing your destiny, chasing your dreams down and stopping at nothing to see them fulfilled. Becoming a mother was like leaving behind my ego and marrying compassion and love and fragility. It was realizing that we never know what the hell is going to happen to us but it's the surprises that have infinite potential to change our lives. I was happy to say goodbye to the notion that all this life is about is me, and say hello to a life of service to my babies, my partner, my family. Shedding my selfish skin was cathartic, and that first month was when I truly shined in my new Technicolor dream coat. Motherhood gave me back myself, in a bright new shade of love and kindness and humility. And living in that limbo our first month together is one of the greatest gifts this motherhood journey has given me yet.

I am tender
I am soft
I am needing
I am fragile

Piper was born the day after Thanksgiving. It was one of those days that feels like a Sunday afternoon. The sun was low, warm and droopy. We took a walk that morning to breakfast, slow and steady, enjoying the day, knowing life was stirring to emerge.

Over eggs, tears began to flow as rushes began to immerse my body. Little rhythms, again and again. The waiter told the cook and the cook told the owner and the people next to us said: "time to go home, eh?" And I said not yet, I'm finishing my toast.

There was never a moment where I said, "this is it." I didn't need to. It was all instinctual, all knowing, as if I'd been here time and time again.

My water broke on that walk home, I was full of toast and eggs and promise.

At home I labored with my 12 year old daughter as my doula, while my husband filled the pool. At 12:30, my midwife and mother arrived just as I was in the sweetest spot, transition.

I birthed Piper in warm water, on all fours, clutching my daughter, my mom and my husband's hand as I roared her earth side at 1:02 pm.

What happened next is most important, though.

After climbing into bed with my husband, my midwifes surrounded us to weigh and stitch and feed and massage and smile and love us. There is barely a word in the English language that can best describe real, true, raw, postpartum care. As one midwife warmed up leftover turkey, the other started our placenta encapsulation. No one left until the sun went down and they arrived again the day after. When one showed up five days in the thick of it, she let me weep on her and sat on my bed, walking me through every prickly feeling, every tender spot, and every question I had.

We, as mothers, are so strong. We are such a force of creation, we are relentless, and magnificent, and we are so able. But, in all my years, I never felt the ability to just lay down and say I am tender, I am soft, I am needing, I am fragile; and in those first postpartum days, I was opened up, stripped of the feeling to always be "okay" and it was the work of those midwifes that allowed me to find myself again, and again during those first few postpartum weeks.

Postpartum care should be a priority for all women. I feel an immeasurable amount of gratitude for the compassion and service I was given, and I believe that all women, no matter where they birth, deserve the grace and attention of a postpartum doula or midwife. You are worth it, our babies are worth it, we are all worth it.

The weather today, and like most days since you were born, has woven in and out of storms and sunshine. Now I cover your sleeping head as a few small drops begin to spit through the sun and clouds. I hear a passing dog walker ask the neighbor about her recent birth, and though I haven't met her yet, I long for a connection. She's probably got her little girl cozied up to her breast just like you are to mine, feeling a multitude of emotions. You are 19 days old my beauty. Even though you have joined us and breathe this air with us, I feel underwater with you. Relearning how to breathe, how to sleep, how to walk with my new hips, how to see through the softness and overwhelmedness in my heart. How to do it all in the name of motherhood. This motherhood that now proceeds my name, my body, my spirit. You are immense. You fill me immensely. I never imagined this kind of washing over. My boy. You are fed and warm and loved and cooed at and always being touched. But all parts of my insides are confused at the utter mess I feel.

but I forgot
to prepare
for the joy.

In my last month of being pregnant, I read every birth story and scrap of advice for new moms that I could find. I tucked away bits of wisdom about birth and how to cope with the pain; I made note of the ways they said my marriage would change once our son was born; I luxuriated in long showers, anticipating that I'd miss them. I looked at pictures of squishy new babes and tried to imagine holding my son in my arms. I worried that I'd experience those baby blues, or their darker relative, postpartum depression. I tried to brace myself for the sleeplessness, for the endlessness of a newborn crying, for the strain it would put on my marriage. I tried not to worry about the pain I knew would come with the unmedicated labor I wanted. I was as prepared as I could be for the difficulty of new motherhood. I was realistic, I thought.

But I forgot to prepare for the joy.

I have long since forgotten any details of labor. I remember the pain in a sort of vague way, like when you have a weird dream and wake up and tell your partner, but the next day all you remember is telling it, not dreaming it. What I do remember and will never forget is when my midwife told me to reach down and pull my son out. As I wrapped my hands around his warm, slippery body, his eyes opened. I pulled him up to cradle him on my belly, the umbilical cord too short to bring him up further, and I felt the pain pour out of my body like water. "Hi baby, hi baby, I'm your mom, it's me, I'm your mom!" was all I could say, over and over.

Later that night, while everyone else slept, my son lay in my arms, wide awake for the longest time, and just stared at me. His eyes moved slowly around my face, memorizing me, and I memorized him. The incredible completeness I felt, the love so powerful that if I stopped to think about it I began to cry, was not a part of my understanding of new motherhood. In my determination to be prepared, to be realistic, I had focused so much on the future difficulty that I had not considered the future joy.

Although, I don't know if I could have been prepared for this. The way my sweet son looks at me like I am the sun and the moon and all the stars - I couldn't have ever understood that until I felt it. The way he soothes when he latches on to nurse, the tension releasing from his body and a sigh of contentment escaping him; his wiggles of pure delight when he wakes up each morning to find me there next to him. I was not prepared for that.

Motherhood is the most beautiful thing I've ever been a part of.

I have heard it said that "a mother knows."

I have a clear and profound memory of watching my mother cut apples for a pie as a child. I stood, entangled in her dress, mesmerized. holding the apple in her left hand, she used what seemed a dangerously sharp knife to slice bits into a bowl. Sword wielder, she! What magic! I thought, in awe of her wound-free hands. How was this possible? She moved so quickly, knowing. She slipped me a slice, knowing. Her legs were strong and firmly planted, knowing. She winked at me, knowing.

I came to my own knowledge less effortlessly. I limped into awareness, desperately clinging to my oblivion.

When I told him about the baby, I recall my body tightening. I can remember standing in front of him and saying quite calmly, "It's okay if you don't want to do this." His aversion to having children well-documented, I was prepared for the possibility that he'd pack his bags that second and bolt for the door. I was encouraged by his wanting to call his sister and share the news.

Despite his protestations, I always believed he had within himself a soul suited to fatherhood. His own father was a hard, Navy man. Bobby had been a Vietnam vet, a machinist, and, in his worst moments, an abuser. This had confused my love as a child and plagued him as a man. In contrast, he was gentle handed, playful, sweet, and carefree. He loved a laughing fit and had sparkling eyes that pierced to my core. He was a lover of life and, quite deeply, of me. His unwillingness to add father to his credentials seemed to come from a fear of what he'd become. As if Bobby was lurking deep down in the creases of his spirit, watching and waiting to pounce. As if a child would unleash this monster within. I hoped instead it would release a dormant moonbeam, radiating warm vibrations through his fingertips and opening paths to renewal. Perhaps we choose which truth we will manifest.

As we told his sister the news, I remember him pouring shots of whiskey. We New Orleans folk stay well lubricated, but his drinking was different. It was a mission. A steam engine with no brakes plowing through towns and leaving rubble in its wake. His drinking had caused us a great deal of strife in the past and I, like many women before me, hid a secret sorrow from friends, family, and chiefly myself. I rationalized the late nights and erratic lifestyle. I embraced my solitude, reading books and daydreaming with abandon. I'd write in my journals and lunch with friends. I watched cheesy romantic comedies and played dress up like a school girl. I grew to expect the distance and separate journeys. It kept a bit of excitement in the reunited moments, and I never doubted his fidelity. Besides, he could always stop if he wanted to, he'd remind me. I would sit after he left for the bar some nights wondering when I'd muster the courage to ask why he didn't want to? The shots flowed freely that evening. I lost count after seven as we hung up with Sissy.

The first week was a blur of a bender. Alcohol can poison the mind. vitriol poured out of his mouth as liquor poured in. How could I have changed so irrevocably the landscape of our lives? Didn't I see the damage I had done? "It's ok if you don't want to do this," I would say meekly, accepting and piling the blame onto my steadily growing weight. I could feel my body tense again as I prepped for the inevitable. I was certain he'd be leaving. I had, many times over the years, resigned myself to the knowledge that our love story would be full of bumps and struggles. I love him fiercely. Our good times were passionately, hysterically, wildly good, and I felt proud to be his woman. Our sweet moments floored me, and the overwhelming power of my love for him brought me again and again to my knees. I built an altar for the man in my heart and prayed at it daily. As I had done so many times, I convinced myself that this would pass. I clung to the notion that, with time, his fear would subside. Our love would overpower his doubt. Our child would replenish us.

In the weeks that followed, he sought balance. In his routine, benders lead to sadness and apologies which leads to soul-searching and calls to the heavens for help to stay sober before the confidence returns and cockiness takes over, driving him out of my arms and our home, and back into the smoky night. "It's okay if you don't want to do this," I'd remind him, my body tight, silently begging him to snap out of it. Desperate he'd hear my mental pleas for peace and calm. Hopeful he'd tame that Bobby beast and the self-doubt that possessed him. Eager for the father he could be to swoop in like a Pegasus, majestic and proud. The wishing was my routine. Wishing it would be over, wishing it was the last time, wishing my doubt away.

That first month of motherhood - my first weeks aware of the precious jewel growing inside me - was eerily similar to the years that preceded it. The first month was much like the remaining months of pregnancy. That first month was exactly like the first month with my darling girl earth side. That first month was like the first six months as a fragile family, until finally I stopped telling him, "It's ok if you don't want to do this."

Instead, I told myself, and my tight, aching body released.

I do not wish to demonize my daughter's father, nor do I fault him for an addiction beyond his control, but a mother just knows. The shift from one to two was instantaneous. Honoring that truth took time and sacrifice.

I look back on my mother cutting apples in the kitchen. She didn't have a superpower or ninja-like skill. She, mother, mama, mommy, she had a job to do and she did it precisely, carefully, smoothly, with her child looking on enraptured. I hope to be that for my daughter. I hope she looks at me and sees not my faltering steps out the door. I hope she doesn't hear my crying in the bathroom or sense my longing to be held. I hope she feels the softness of my legs as she wraps herself around them, clinging to my skirt, hungry for my attention, watchful of my actions. I hope she remembers ease and comfort and closeness.

Like alcohol, motherhood changes a person. Motherhood emboldened me to be the best version of myself. Motherhood doubled my focus and narrowed my gaze. Motherhood makes the other times seem less than. Motherhood is the best party with the best people, and it goes from dusk until dawn. Like him, I don't want to stop. I love this life I'm living. I choose it. I am mother to a magical, observant, investigative, joyful girl child, and blessed to be. The universe has provided me with a soul to nurture and guide and adore with all my might. My purpose has been defined, and I am reborn. I don't know much, but I do know that.

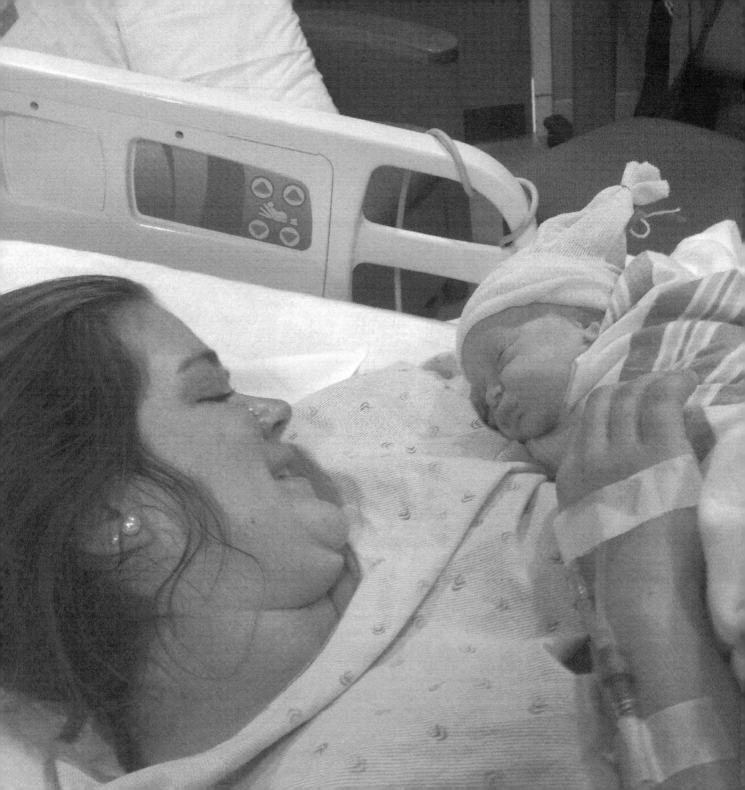

The first month. Love and lost expectations. So much damn love. Milk that took forever to come in and embarrassing acceptance of donations and waiting. And so much love that I almost forgot all of it. The anxiety of Bilirubin levels and IV's and incubators and praying. First visits with Santa with so many wires hidden under your blanket and puffy faces from crying. I have never cried and hit my knees to pray until that night. And then you got better and all the diaper changes through the incubator holes and the first few postpartum days spent in the hospital without showers so I didn't leave your side were obsolete. A car ride home, terrified thatI buckled you in too tight and calm that you were actually in my car. Walking inside behind your father carrying you sleeping and bundled up so warm and cozy and the snowflakes falling so calmly. A dream come true.

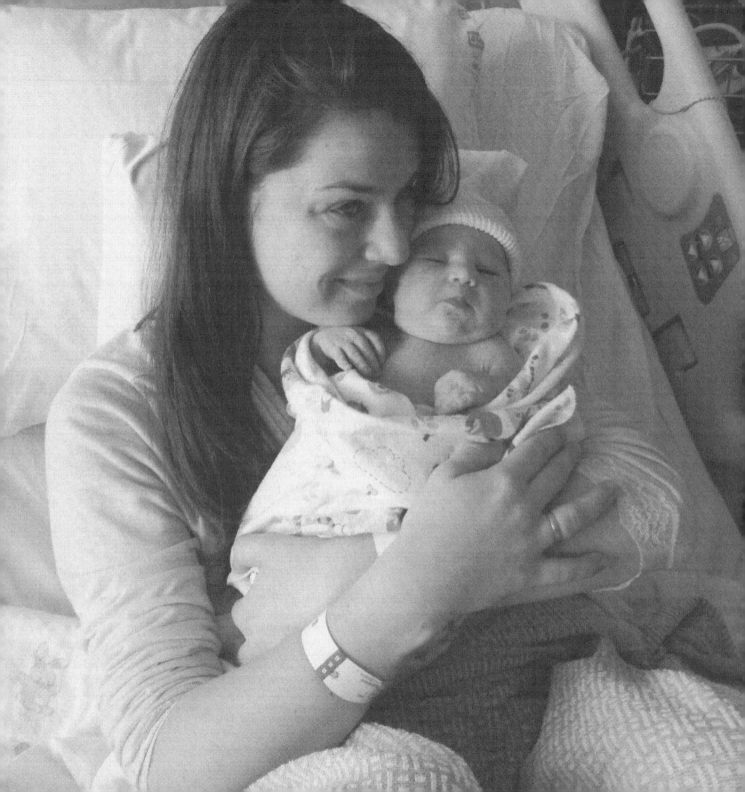

It was 5 in the morning. The little one had been up most of the night, fussing and letting me know what she thought of the crib in which we put her in. I must have gotten up 500 times that night to soothe her and after a certain point, I just collapsed on the floor in her nursery, unable to make the 10 steps back to our bedroom. I was 6 days postpartum and everything had taken a toll on my body. The labor, the recovery, the excess fluids in my body (which were STILL there), the roller-coaster of emotions, the upcoming visitors, and the baby. The thought of walking back to my bedroom only to get up yet again was enough to knock me to the floor.

When she woke up again, like I knew she would, something inside me snapped. I felt the frustration before I even opened my eyes. I picked her up and tried my best to soothe her by rocking and swaying gently across the room. Her cries got louder, and I could feel the dark frustration dangerously bubbling to the surface. I took a deep breath and continued swaying, focusing on keeping my energy positive so that she didn't pick up on the negativity. Even louder cries. It's like she knew that I was hiding something. She was frustrated that I was not being true to myself, to that moment and emotion that I was feeling.

I clutched her into my arms and ran down our short hallway, towards the bedroom where my husband slept peacefully. I ripped the door open and screamed, "Jay, take her away from me!"

He instantly leapt out of bed, and took her from my arms as I ran towards our bathroom. I gripped the sink with my sweaty fingers and the heavens opened. Tears came spilling out, so fast that my knees buckled. I cried with my whole body. I cried so hard that I convulsed, each jerk of my shoulders and back bringing in a new crop of tears. I cried a tear for every mother that has found herself in a similar situation but was unable to release, to feel this moment and truly embrace it.

I could have cried forever, and I still do when I think about that single moment, a moment out of a million in my journey to motherhood.

lost and
present and
living in wonder.

I've been wholly and completely changed since you came into the world. Different entirely, in body, mind, and spirit.

I woke up nearly forty-eight hours after giving birth and walked into the bathroom. The woman looking back at me from the mirror was worn and awful and I hardly recognized her sunken face. She shed nearly thirty pounds overnight, and the sudden change in weight and shape, along with the searing pain between her hips, was causing her to stand with a dramatic lean in her spine. Crooked like an old woman, rail thin, like she was as a girl. Her hair was wild and still sweat stained from labor.

But pained as she was, I marveled at this woman. For she was completely foreign to me. And though I knew I was looking at the same physical form that I've hauled around for twenty-two years, I still felt that I was seeing myself for the very first time. And I was.

I am a new being.

The woman I was on September 26th has passed away, just like I expected that she would. And though wildly unfamiliar yet, this new form that I've taken on is something ancient, and comfortable. It's what I was supposed to become, I think, right from the very beginning.

It's hard to describe, this change. I'm no longer living in one body - my soul has split into two. I guess I feel a bit like a child myself. Lost and present and living in wonder.

I took a walk outside the apartment last night, alone for the first time since you were born. It's Autumn now, but in Texas it still has that very late summer feel, like apples and fireflies and night skies fit for stargazing. I slipped my shoes off and walked in the grass, and I swore for a moment that I was ten years old again, and it was almost dark out, the streetlights all just coming on, and I would hear the sound of a screen door slamming from down the street, my mother calling me home from somewhere far off. I would run, run, over the freshly mowed lawns between the neighbor's house and my own, all the while judging the time by the sweet cool hair of the Earth beneath my feet.

I can't wait to learn about this new woman. I can't wait to learn about you, my love. We are making magic together already, the three of us, your father, and you, and I. Children again, growing older, living in constant wonder. Watching, waiting, holding our breath.

it felt like
maybe my skin
would one day
begin to feel
like it belonged
to me again.

I was never afraid of my body. I was never cautious or inhibited by the pleasure and energy I could harness and give out. I was always moving, always gliding through dark and damp nights, with indigo speckled lights dotted randomly through my vision. I slinked and slid from one body to another, spending each morning in a new persons vacant side of the bed. Everyone warned me I'd feel hollow or empty, but I never did. I felt free and full and so very comfortable in this life I was gliding in.

Then, one Tuesday, a tiny little black smudge, no bigger than a kidney bean, appeared on a grey crackly screen in a dark room in a Planned Parenthood. It looked like something ancient, something powerful and cosmic and so very far away, and yet it was happening, right in front of me, hidden beneath me. I didn't even know who you were. I didn't even know whose you were. I still don't.

I'm so sorry.

When you were born, midwife occupied in the hall, doctor on call at home, I pulled you from the dark and damp room within me, all alone, unassisted, and terrified. When you surfaced and I looked into your eyes, it simply didn't matter whose you were, because you were all mine. So small, and so perfect and completely daunting. The idea that you had come from inside me was both surreal and horrifying. I didn't think we'd be okay. You kept crying, and I kept crying, wishing someone would take you from my arms while they stitched me up, but I kept getting told it was normal and this is what happens and that at 3pm the next day, I'd have to go home.

For the first time in my life, I was frightened of my body. Frightened of what I could do and frightened of the amount of bone splitting pain I could endure without completely dissolving and diffusing. I was a broken soul in a foreign body. This mother's skin I had been thrust into was so unfamiliar to me, and all day I had milk curdling under my clothes, knots of lint and spit up in my hair and purple rings bigger than Saturn's orbiting under my eyes.

This is not who I was, this mother, yet there you were, completely reliant on me to smile and wear this new skin I was reborn into. You were real living proof for everyone else around me to say, "Look, that's yours. She's your daughter, and you are her mother. Suck it up." But I refused.

I'm so sorry.

You were so perfect, so fair and pretty and all I could think was this is not me, this is not mine, I am not this and this is your fault. I didn't want to nurse you because you hurt me. My perfect white creamy breasts that were once only ever softly caressed and admired were now demanded and grabbed by sticky hands and sharp fingernails and sucked raw and dry. Why did I deserve this?

1 month after you were born, I was determined. Determined to shed you and this skin you'd forced me to wear. I hired a baby-sitter, taught her how to mix formula, and left. That night was the first time I had sex after I had you, and I screamed. I screamed until my throat bled, and then after, so did my vagina. I felt more pain then I had ever felt before. This was not how my body was meant to be treated. When I birthed you in that hospital, at 1:12am, it was painful, yes. But I had you to show for it. Even though you were proof I had to be a mother, you were proof to me that I could have a baby.

When it was over, I didn't sleep beside him. Instead I came home and found you, breathing peacefully and quietly on the vacant side of my bed. I crept in beside you, and kissed your honey hair, and surrendered. I surrendered to everything you made me into. I surrendered to the idea that I am someones mother, and that is more than I have ever been before. I surrendered to the cold fact that my vagina is never going to look, feel, and behave the same as it did before, but my womb kept you warm for 9 months, and that's pretty brilliant. And I surrendered to the reality that I needed you, as much as you needed me, and that we are in this world together. That night, as I lay wide awake beside you, stars flooding through your veins, my skin began to feel a bit tighter, and a bit more tailored. It felt like maybe my skin would one day feel like it belonged to me again.

I sit on the metal table in the OR, my bare back hunched over, waiting for the anesthesiologist to insert the spinal block. My husband, my rock, isn't allowed into the room until this part is over, so I clutch the nurse's outstretched arms instead. Anxiety leaps from my body, sending my extremities shaking, my teeth chattering. The nurse notices and whispers, "Take deep breaths, hun. Everything will be okay." Tears prick my eyes. I feel more like a scared child than a strong mother about to give birth.

My son entered the world via c-section, in a flurry of bright lights, rubber gloves, and loud noises. My natural birth plan was shattered because he was a big boy (9 pounds) and my body didn't progress the way my doctor wanted. My baby was removed from my body and whisked away. I couldn't see him, but I heard his tiny cries. The IV medications made me vomit while my doctor stapled my new postpartum body shut. I felt helpless and empty until I saw Julian's beautiful chubby pink face. The memory of seeing this perfect new being will forever be tucked away in my heart.

The first month was the most difficult of my 27 years. My heart was full, but my world was unrecognizable. I desperately wanted to breastfeed. Nurses at the hospital tried to help us, but within 24 hours my nipples were bruised and bleeding. I developed mastitis in both breasts. I sought out lactation nurses, but my son kept losing weight. At the advice of our pediatrician, I switched him to formula and ceased breastfeeding. My mind went to dark places. I felt like a failure and those feelings swept over me amidst the sleepless nights, the mastitis fevers, the pain of my c-section scar. Every time a visitor came to meet Julian I inexplicably burst into tears as soon as they left. Rivers of tears were shed over those uncertain weeks.

Now I look back on that first month with clarity. I should have reached out for more help, should have been more gentle with myself, should have realized how strong I truly was. Julian is now a one-year-old boy who is my moon and stars, my entire world wrapped up in a squishy toddler body. We're still figuring this whole life thing out, and with enough love and gentleness, I know everything will be okay.

My milk came in at midnight on the third day. I sat straight up in the sheets and cried out, my arms crossed against my breasts. It was liquid fire flowing down from within me. My skin stretched around a chest so swollen, so full, so foreign that it was no longer my own. Milk ran down and pooled underneath the loose skin of my stomach. My husband woke and I told him to go back to sleep, please, not to look at me when I was so awful, all covered in sour sticky liquid and sweat from a southern summer half-sleep. I tried to latch Aspen to one of my breasts but she choked and gagged on the flow of milk. No one ever told me that my milk would arrive so suddenly, so terribly, and I held the squirming babe to my damp night shirt and wept, for the ache in my breast was worse than the pains of labor. More than anything, I wanted someone to talk to. Someone who understood, who had been covered in milk before, who could help me to wash the sheets and wash my tacky skin and teach me how to properly nurse my child. But there was no one, so I woke my husband, and when he finally opened his eyes and asked, "What is it, what's wrong?" I wiped my eyes and rocked the baby and answered, "Nothing, I'm sorry, go back to sleep."

We are so otherworldly, you and I. You take me to other realms with just the sound of your breath and the feel of your sweet soft skin. You remind me who I really am: a divine woman, who has nurtured life in many lifetimes, some in this world, some in others, on timelines before and after this one, some simultaneously occurring with this moment. I am Mother Nature in all her forms, and my current favorite is this one, being this woman, your mother in this wild world at this crazy time. Settling into this moment, right here right now, cuddled up with you, my lovely daughter, is precious beyond measure. Time and space have nothin' on my love for you.

Last night I was making coffee (because coffee after seven in the evening has become a postpartum ritual of sorts) and you were watching Aspen when I heard her little head hit the carpet. She had been sitting proper between your feet, and some flailing bit of excitement had made her fall backwards. She wasn't hurt, but I was angry at you for watching your phone rather than your daughter, so I snatched her up from the floor and held her to my chest like a stolen diamond.

"You're not allowed to watch her any more," I said, and then spit a venomous "ever!" just to make sure I had been clear.

You were standing already, arms out, reaching for her, but I held her closer still. "Why not?"

"Because! You don't watch her watch her. You have to look at her and see what she's doing and make sure she's not going to fall off a fucking cliff or something."

"Look at her!" you pointed, "She's fine!"

"That's not the point!"

You sat back on the couch and froze over, like you sometimes do, your face ripe with pain and flushed with thought. After a minute, an hour, a day, I threw a pink rubber block at your chest. "Hey! Talk to me!"

"You've been so upset with me lately! I feel like an awful father. Not at all like my dad was. Like I'm not the father you wanted me to be. You wanted the baby --"

"I wanted her? So does that mean you didn't?" I cut him short. Aspen laughed at something on the wall, and I started to cry.

"God, no!" you said, "I'm just so young. I don't even have my own shit figured out. Maybe if we'd waited, maybe if I was older, was more mature, I don't know. Maybe I would be better. It used to just be us, you know? And we never fought. Not until we had a baby. And I'm not blaming her. It just upsets me that you're so angry with me all the time now, and I don't know what I can do to make you happy."

I sat down on the couch with the baby in my arms and watched her swallow the living room with her eyes. She didn't need much these days, milk every so often, a rock to sleep, my arms, my breasts, and in that moment I felt that I needed everything from you -- even the things you couldn't possibly give me. "I'm sorry," I said.

"You're not though." you fumbled at the buckle on your pants.

"I am! I'm sorry. Do you think this is easy for me? That it isn't a big change for me, too?" I swallowed. I thought to tell you that you should leave, that you should go live your life, the one you were missing, the one we chose to skip by getting married at 19, by having a babe at 21, but I knew that would only cut you deeper. I swallowed again. Thought of the truth, and how bitter it was in my mouth, but I said it anyway. "You have to understand than I'm broken in so many ways. I've been on edge, and it's not your fault, and it's not her's either. I think it's because I'm being torn in so many directions now."

"How so?"

"It used to just be me, and I took care of myself, and then it was you and I, and I was able to give you all of me, to touch you and love you and be entirely yours, and I miss that so fucking much, because now I have to care for me, and for you, and for her, and as much as I want to touch and fuck like we used to, I can't do that anymore."

I was sobbing. Aspen watched me from my arms, smiling. I caught my breath, continued, "I'm grieving the life I used to have, even though I chose to leave it, and because of that I'm more upset than I should be over things that don't matter. I'm still the same woman I was before I became a mother. Somewhere, she's in there, but she's dying, KC. Half of me is dying."

You sat back against the sofa and your face softened, and I knew that you understood. Maybe not entirely, but enough to know that we were both hurting, that we were both trying, that we were both changed in the most profound way that a person can be changed.

Later on, after Aspen had gone to bed, we made popcorn to eat with our coffee and laughed about how wild it would be if we hadn't talked things through. If we had stayed silent and sour and wondering why the other was so bruised. "That's how people fall apart," I had nodded, and you agreed.

And with coffee and sugar and butter and salt, with love and old hands and new skin and pink rubber blocks, for now, my love, we stay together.

I could watch you for hours, your tiny delicate body buried into his, into the same warming shoulders my head collapsed onto under every moon and reached for with every rising sun. Hypnotized by his heartbeat and comforted by his scent, that heavenly scent that whispers to your heart 'you're home,' and removes the rest of the world from around you. And every fiber of me dances knowing you feel it too, the same endless love and comfort from being in his arms as I do with them wrapped around me.

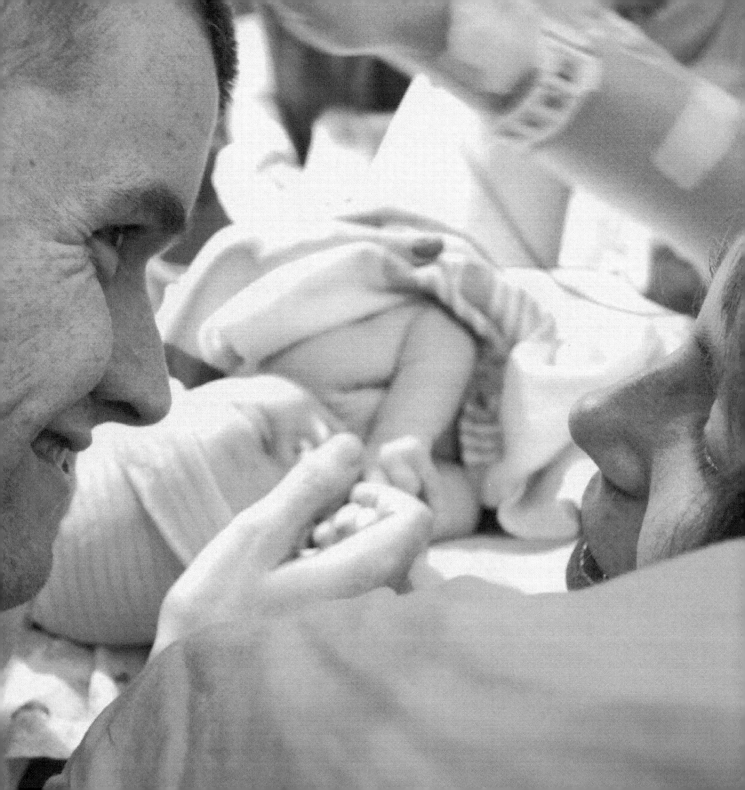

but then,
we come
together again.

I sat on the couch with the babe on my knees, slapping his little feet together, kissing the tip of his nose, savoring every little giggle he released. My husband had slipped away for a bit to take out the trash, so the house was still and quiet. He returned quickly and suddenly, reaching his hand out for mine, gently grabbing my shoulder instead.

"Come outside with me. Please?"

I stood, moving the babe to my hip, pulling my blouse a little tighter to brace myself for the evening chill. I noticed the sky from beyond the glass door, and I knew immediately what he wanted. The soft afternoon blue had spilled into a vivid watercolor chaos, blanketing the sky. It was so beautiful - a different view each way I turned. He searched for my hand, lacing his fingers with mine, smiling gently. Frogs chirped in the distance, the air grew cold, and we stood closely together in admiration until the night finally fell and the moon peeked out from behind the fog. We found peace in the stillness. We found joy in something as simple as the setting sun and departing day.

Sometimes days are really hard. Sometimes our bodies feel foreign, our minds are cluttered, and we have no real sense of direction from the overwhelming confusion of taking on a new life. Not just that of the baby, but the new life, the new self, within us. We were born too, in that hospital room, and some days it's hard to grasp. We are the same, but different. Worn ragged and raw, expected to know everything and needing to be everything and so much more for a tiny human, and for each other. Some days, it's really, really hard.

Sometimes we fight. Sometimes we not only resent our selves, but we resent each other. Some days we are nestled underneath the same sheets, but we're miles apart. Some days, we're not even that close.

But then, we come together again, crashing and collapsing into one another, sobbing and broken, and somehow - in spite of everything - we become whole again. We remember that we still, and will always, have each other to run to when the sun sets on another day. We have seen each other in our most ugly, broken state before, and we were able to find light within the hardened ash.

Parenting is not easy, or glamorous, but God, it's so damn rewarding, and euphoric, and utter and complete bliss. It's a true miracle of the universe, the gift of all gifts. We look at him, and we can't believe just how much love we hold within us. We stumble, but with scraped up knees and shaking legs, we push forward - together. Always, somehow, together. I squeezed his hand a little tighter, feeling his gaze upon me, his smile warming my heart. In that moment - in every moment - I couldn't imagine my life without him. Through it all, I wouldn't ever want to do this crazy parenting thing with anyone else

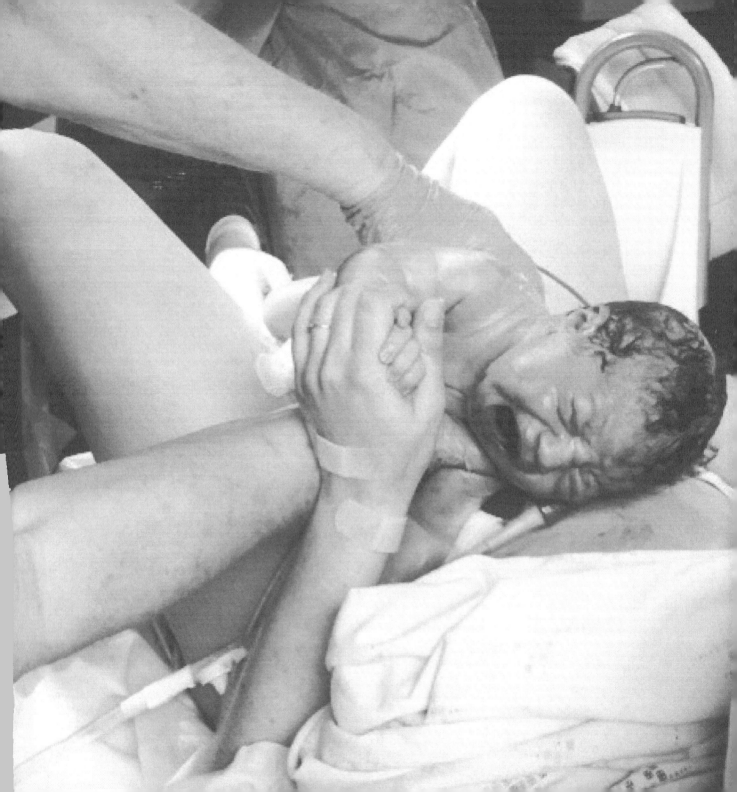

my increasing
confidence
enabled her
happiness,
and, as such,
she enabled mine.

When I first became a mother, I was overcome by feelings of inadequacy. The thought of changing a diaper brought me to tears for fear of doing it wrong and causing my sweet baby girl, Lorelei, any pain whatsoever. Nursing caused me to scream every form of profanity with which I was familiar, crying and gritting my teeth through every bad latching attempt. I have grateful memories of my husband and mother helping me lift my bleeding breast to Lorelei's mouth so that I could clench my fists and cry on their shoulders. Lorelei's sucking hurt more than any other hurt I've ever felt, but my will to do what was best for her gave me just enough strength to provide her with nourishment every few hours, day and night.

Eventually, my nipples became numb and the amount of milk leaking from them lessened. Lorelei, who for a period of time cried for hours on end every single day, finally began to see that life was more than discomfort and a screaming mother who reeked of fear and second guesses. I was able to comfort her without worrying about whether or not I was doing anything right, and she was able to be a joyous baby, full of wonder and a willingness to experience life outside of the uterine nest in which she first developed. My increasing confidence enabled her happiness, and, as such, she enabled mine.

The feeling of being needed by a tiny human being who had an entire lifetime ahead of her was so profound that my life's path changed. Because of this baby that I brought into the world with my own body, whose strength I had only recently become aware of, I decided to dedicate my life to helping other mothers both before and after they give birth to babies of their own. Lorelei was inspiration in its purest form, and she remains to be so at the age of two, as is her three-month-old baby sister, Isla, who has been lucky enough to experience Confident Mama from the very beginning.

None of this would have come forth if it weren't for my supportive husband, who had yet to marry me when Lorelei arrived earthside. His willingness to do everything I couldn't for that first month is what allowed the mother within me to emerge. He stayed awake with Lorelei during her difficult nights; he changed the majority of the diapers; and he supported the two of us without once letting on that was bothered or overwhelmed. If it weren't for his selfless, caring nature and understanding of what I was going through both mentally and physically, the best parts of me would never have grown to accommodate the needs of the new person I've become, nor those of the two new people that we created. It is because of him that I adapted, and it is because of our two daughters that I have grown capable of embracing and loving the living of life.

Last night was amazing. Noah behaved like a grownup; asked to eat, kindly-nicely, three times between 10 pm and 7 am. besides that, we slept through the darkness. I haven't felt this fresh ever since he was born.

We tend to share the generally pretty moments in our lives around here, but I must take a pause and notice on how really hard it is to be mama to such a tiny being. The complete exhaustion from not sleeping, and (as my mother says) "working in the mine" (aka breast-feeding) the whole day are just things to get used to physically. What goes on in my mind and heart in the meantime are what really matter. I exist in two bodies, I feel with two hearts. my emotions hit high ups and lows easily under a minute by his smile and his cry. There never was another man who made me feel so loved, needed, and helpless in the same time. not being able to understand every single sign he sends me breaks me into pieces, and brings me to unchain the weaknesses I couldn't have solved without him. The rules I built with oh so much attention to make my life, they slowly transform into something new, much more honest, and beautiful. Along the way though, it's hard work. A battle with my ego every day. An ongoing conversation between the old me and the new.

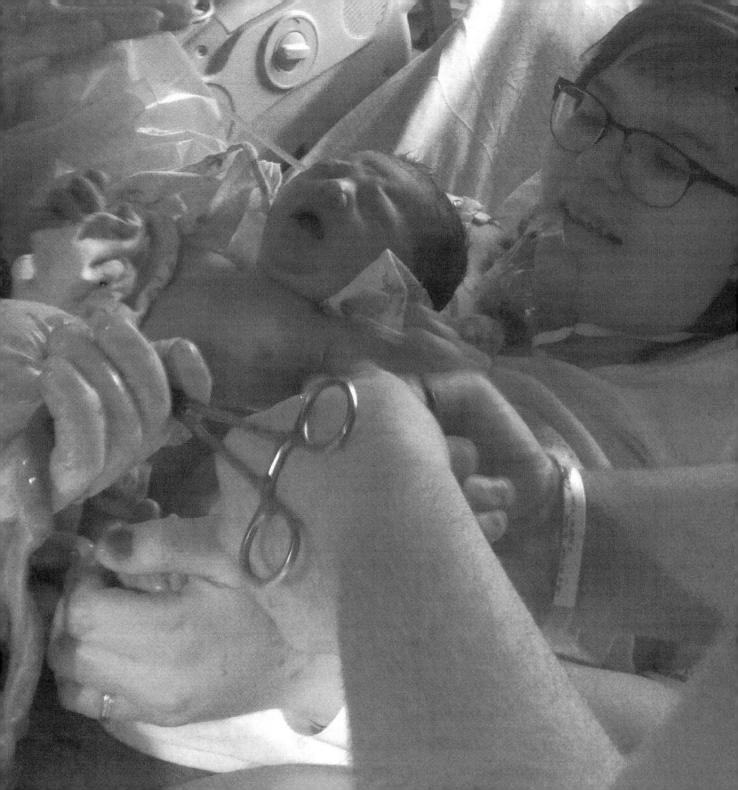

From the moment she was born, I knew I would do everything I could to protect her and provide for her, but it took time to get to know her and fall madly in love with her.

The first night home from the hospital she was crying and hungry, I put her to my breast and I cried as she latched on. My nipples were on fire and ached with each gulp of colostrum.

I remember thinking, "I can't do this. I'm not strong enough."

I quickly unlatched her and we both sat there and cried together. Feeling defeated, exhausted and helpless to feed my child, I cried my way into the kitchen. I warmed a bottle of some sample formula my mother had gave me. It smelled so weird, and looked nothing like the colostrum I had fed her while in the hospital. Hot tears ran down my face as I brought the bottle back to our bedroom, and I wept as she refused to take a single drop of it.

It was in that moment I realized I had to surrender. I understood that feeding my child would be painful for me, but it was what she needed. It was something I had to do. I put my babe back to my breast, bite my lip and silently cried while she nursed herself to sleep. As I laid there holding my sleeping child in my arms, I was filled with a mixture of exhaustion and extreme pride.

It was a strange kind of bliss. A feeling you can't quite put into words. It was this sacrifice of self that initiated me into the sacred circle we call motherhood.

a glorious mess,
I thought.

I love being a parent. But saying that doesn't mean it's been easy. During the first week of nursing a newborn, I hit blissful highs and tearful lows. At one point, pinned to a rocking chair in our once tidy bedroom upstairs, I relished in the empty bowls and crumpled sheets, the spit up cloths and bountiful pillows that mounted our bed. A glorious mess, I thought. Something was happening in our house. All was full of life.

A few days later, pinned to the couch, nursing a newborn, I felt like my only redeeming quality was breast milk. I didn't understand then that everything would change. That it wouldn't always feel so constant, so exhausting. That my baby wouldn't always nurse for an hour at a time, every hour. That I would one day have longer breaks, that one day I won't be nursing him at all. Yes, babies grow into toddlers, into children, into teens, into adults. Realizing this constant movement means I can let go whilst simultaneously treasuring the magnitude of Now.

What I didn't expect to be so challenging is the adjustment we have had to embrace in our relationship as husband and wife, lover and lover. I had heard glimmers of this truth in passing, picked up from segments of documentaries we watched, skimming over that section. That won't happen to us. How unfortunate. I remember Isaac saying, I won't be your number one any more. It broke my heart and I didn't want it to be true.

It is true.

Becoming a mother means shifting from Nymphette to Guardian of the Wellbeing of a Vulnerable Life. It means balancing five spinning plates whilst juggling on your toes. It means online shopping late at night and wearing a baby most of the day, leaving dishes undone and wet washing in the basket. It means realizing that you are a human being who needs to be touched, but not too much! It means accepting that you cannot give it all, that you cannot please everyone, that your back will hurt, your wrists will hurt, your shoulders will hurt, but they will get stronger. You will get spit up in your hair, bright orange, turmeric-colored baby poop on your clothes. You will wake up during the night and develop new ways of entertaining a constantly evolving human.

You will learn to be spontaneous. You will learn to be responsive, response-able. You will learn how to wear your baby because it's best for them and you. You will go for long stretches without food without realizing. You may get incredibly thirsty (and soaking wet) from breastfeeding. It's likely that you will love your body more after giving birth – mostly because of the respect you will feel for it, producing and then nourishing your incredible new baby. You won't ever have the same body again. You won't ever have the same relationship again. You will probably mourn this. You might celebrate this.

I was surprised at how much things changed. But they keep changing.

How do we lovers cope with this unspoken shift, the changing of the spotlight from each other, towards the gaze of a creature you would do anything for? I have wept inexplicable tears whilst looking at my son. The love I feel for him is frustratingly indescribable. But the love I have for Isaac? It feeds me. You will need to be fed. Your partner may feel isolated, neglected, far away. Keep communicating, keep sharing how it is for you. If you feel something spiky growing between you, talk about it. Even if you don't have words. Start talking. Just share. You will come together one morning in tears, and together the same night in love.

This is what I've learned it means to be in a partnership, to be a parent. A glorious mess. Constantly evolving. (I will love you forever, Isa.)

At the age of 23 I gave birth to Joy (stillborn at 24 weeks) and at 24 (exactly 1 year after I was supposed to give birth to Joy), to Chloe. Giving birth to Chloe went easily for me. I felt no contractions until the end. My body was back in shape in a few days. Even breastfeeding went perfectly. But, I had a hard time believing this baby was going to stay. I was scared to really love her, that I would have to let her go, too. This unhappy feeling made me feel guilty. What kind of mother isn't able to love her child from the moment she is born? Everything went perfectly, why wasn't I able to be happy like every other mother on earth? My baby girl always cried when she was separated from me. I slept sitting with her in my arms in bed for 6 weeks. During the daytime, I had this fantastic sling. So, for weeks it was like she was literally a part of me again. In time, the confidence that she was going to stay & that I did deserve her came.

I have always known her.

I remember the drive home from the hospital like it was yesterday. The sun gently illuminated Teagan's face as she slept in her car seat, lips gently pursed and face still speckled with dried vernix. I sat in the back seat with her as my husband drove home, more carefully than ever. Like typical overachieving first time parents, we listened to Baby Einstein during the 60-minute ride home. I sat in the back seat, not because Teagan needed me, but because the front seat was too far away.

I was high on motherhood. I was swollen with pride. I was a creator and a goddess and for the first time, felt like my own hero. My body had given us a daughter; we were finally a family. I was wrapped in a thick blanket of unadulterated joy. Yet, underneath, the pit of my stomach was filled with undigested emotion. It sat there, continuing at a slow, rolling boil. I needed a replay of the past 48 hours, where everything is slowed to a near halt. I yearned for time to process how my body had created life, how Teagan had been born in hotel room because my midwife contended I was overreacting to the strength of my still-4-minutes-apart contractions, how quickly the woman I was seemed to have been swallowed whole by the woman who had just birthed my daughter. Only a week prior, with warm hands placed gingerly on my belly, friends told me that I was about to experience the best chapter of my life. Cherish every moment, they advised. Before you know it, she will be in college. What they didn't mention is that early motherhood would tear me in two.

The hardest part about the days as new mother was figuring out how to make sense of my love for my daughter. The walls of my heart had cracked into a thousand pieces when she was born, but I couldn't piece them back together. What I felt for Teagan could not be distilled, described, or tucked away neatly in my heart.

It's a strange thing, to be overwhelmed by love. I can't count the number of times my husband walked into the room to find me staring at Teagan while she slept, weeping quietly. He would ask what was wrong, but there was nothing for me to say. How would anyone understand that I ceased to know myself, that I was crying because I was a mother and my love for my daughter was crippling? One day he sat next to me, put his arm around me as I sobbed, and calmly explained that I was exhibiting some symptoms consistent with postpartum depression. I felt alone in a vast sea of emotion. Only other mothers could help me make sense of the troughs between the waves. As we approach the day that will mark Teagan's first trip around the sun, time has tempered the raw emotion of early motherhood. During periods of a sleeping mind and a dreaming heart, I have realized that my emotional struggle of early motherhood culminated in a single question; how I had ever lived without my daughter. It has taken a year, but I now know the answer.

I have always known her; she has been with me forever.

My son, Bodhi, is 11 months old. His first month seems so long ago. Looking back, I didn't realize the depths of this new person I was becoming. The labor and delivery was all that I thought it would be. Exhilarating, otherworldly, slightly terrifying, painful, and full of relief when over. I remember, at times, feeling totally okay with the experience to begging for anyone to help me by cutting me in half to get him out.

When he was born, my partner and Bodhi's dad, Joshua cried. I looked from Bodhi to Josh with utter amazement and puzzlement. Who was this new human in the room? Holy shit, did that come out of my body? Why am I shaking so badly? Josh is crying, why am I not crying? Should I be crying?

After that it was a sea of changing diapers and feedings. Breastfeeding came somewhat naturally to me. His latch did not, but I just let him plug along anyway. This left me bloody, blistered, and chapped. Feeding my son had me in excruciating pain, and he ate every 1-2 hours. There were times I would sit up in bed with him, no shirt on, breastfeeding and crying. I would look to Josh for help, knowing that he could only offer support and I would just have to suffer through this alone. Sometimes I would be so tired, I would be afraid that I was going to drop Bodhi when caring him to the changing table. I would tell myself, just this one diaper change, just this one feeding, to remind myself to focus on the present, the here and now as to not get overwhelmed.

When I was up at night, walking him around our apartment, singing One Love, I would wonder how many other mothers were up at 3am with their babies, walking in patterns, swaying their babes to sleep. The earth has a different feel. A quiet, stillness at that time. I would tell myself to soak it all in, because it would pass so quickly. And sure enough, it did. Next month, Bodhi will have made one full revolution around the sun.

I wish I could tell you that I don't want to have sex. With you. Or with anybody else. Anymore. Ever.

Hopefully it's temporary. Worst case scenario, it's a part of that ancient instinct of having had a kid and not wanting to have one (or two, or three, or four...) anymore. I remember having bodily desires and feeling sincere pleasure in the simplest act, but then it abruptly stopped the moment I first felt nausea at the beginning of my pregnancy. I didn't know it at that time, but now I realize that it was over for me. At least with you, or at least for a minimum of 3 to 5 years.

However, you didn't nurture a tiny human creature under your heart for 9 months. You didn't birth her. You didn't feed her with your breast milk. You didn't lack sleep, or sanity, or time to yourself. So, I guess after all, it's the ancient instinct which doesn't want to repeat it all over again in the nearest future, even though I love this tiny human being with all my heart.

You could never understand this dilemma of mine. I wish I could tell you, but I won't.

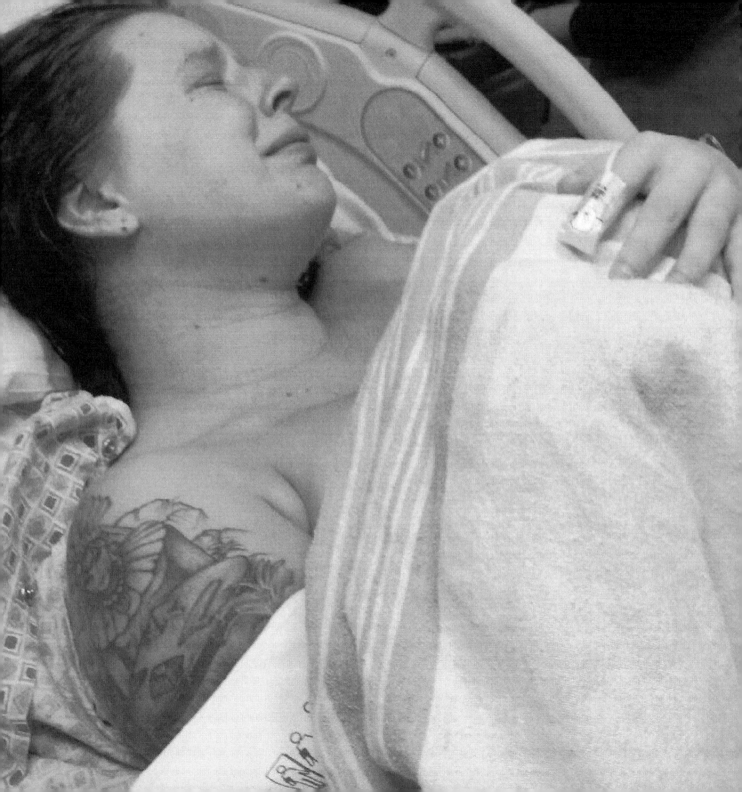

Our bed was so familiar, the sheets were slept in, and the pillow cases falling off the pillows. I remember this bed, I've slept here so many times before. This wasn't the same bed. My body cradles a small body, a new body. Her fingers clenched tightly and her mouth moving as if she were nursing. I feel a calloused hand touch my flabby belly, it's so warm but strange.

"I miss the way we used to be." So badly did I want to roll over and curl into his embrace but I couldn't. His hand slips away from my skin and he turns around; our backs touch.

I had never felt more far away from my lover than I did then. I knew our lives together would be different but I didn't know our bed, our home, and our love would change.

Most of the time I cried, missing the lonely nights alone with our dogs, our legs twined together. I embraced our daughter, the chemical reaction in my body branded me to her but a constant fear of my lover not accepting this life haunted me.

Keeping her tightly in my arms, rocking her to slumber, he found us. He took us into his loving grace. He kissed both of us and I knew. I knew we would be okay.

but I refuse
to forget
about you.

I've been too busy with a babe at my breast to notice that you're feeling lonely. You reach out for me, like you used to, playful and rough-handed in the best possible way, and I tuck away from your touch, because there are other things to do, you know. Because Aspen might wake, or because my skin is too glossy and sour from dried milk, or because there are dishes in the sink, laundry to be folded, hands to wash, bread to bake.

But I'm lucky, because I've felt the weight of loneliness on my shoulders before. I can recognize it, before it gets too heavy to lift.

You took me by the shoulders today and I fell into you and stayed there for a year, it seemed. And I felt then that we were woven so tightly together, and yet we were still fragile, too. It would be far too easy to ignore your loneliness. To tend to the babe and allow you, my love, to shrink down, grow older, grow heavy. I think this happens, sometimes. A child comes, and the love is shifted, shattered, rearranged.

But I refuse to forget about you.

My mother came by today to see Aspen, but the little thing was sleeping soundly in our bed.

"This is good," my mother said, "now you'll have time to wash those dishes in the sink. Maybe pick up a bit, yeah?"

"I could," I said, "But I'd rather spend time with my husband."

She turned her eyes back toward the tower of stained saucers and milk-smeared glass. "When you were a baby, I would get all of my chores done when you were sleeping. Cross things off the to-do list."

And without thinking, I let resentment boil up and bubble over. "And, how did that go for you?" I spat.

"Excuse me?"

I swallowed. "How did that go for you, mom?"

But I don't think she understood. She shrugged. "I got everything done," she said.

When I was a girl, I could feel the weight of my father's loneliness on my skin. From the time I was born (or maybe earlier even - I'll never know), my mother chose chores over the touch of my father's hands. She was always buzzing about, never still, always worried. Forever tending to me, and tending to supper, and tending to the spiderwebs that built up in the peak of the ceiling. But never to him.

And so, he left.

I fell into you today, and I stayed there while the babe slept in the bedroom, while the dishes grew cold in the sink, while the Earth rolled on beneath our feet. I'll never forget about you, my love. And this (oh, this! the feeling of your fingers dancing along my spine! the taste of tobacco lips, your cigar smile! a moment spent, or two, or three, skin to skin, heart to heart!) is how we stay together.

Thirty-four weeks. I wake up and notice I can see my feet again and my clothes are looser. My stomach had shrunk. I call my OBGYN and he kindly but casually suggests I go and see him if I'm worried. I decide I'm being dramatic and carry on getting ready for my sisters wedding rehearsal. But when we are on the highway and about to pass the hospital I tell my husband to pull in.

An hour later, I'm holding my daughter, all two kilograms of her. I'm shaking, crying. What if I hadn't come? She would have died.

And suddenly, I become a victim of my body's chemistry. Anxiety creeps in quickly, ferocious every day. I look at my daughter around the clock. I can't sleep. I can't eat. I just keep replaying the scenario out in my head. What if. What if. What if.

But she is here, they say! Fighting, full of life! I love her so much, but I feel I failed her. I couldn't possibly be enough. Days and nights pass. I lose kilo upon kilo upon kilo. I don't sleep. I just watch her tiny chest rise and fall. Tears fall from my eyes all day long. I barely notice them anymore. My husband creeps out in the middle of the night while I am feeding her, my sobs wake him.

"Baby, you need help. We need help. I'm going to get you help." The relief is instant, and I fall asleep in his arms. We go to the doctor and the words pour out of me. I can't stop. He is old and kind, understanding. He tells me I will feel better within days, but he is wrong. I feel better instantly, just being heard. Just being held.

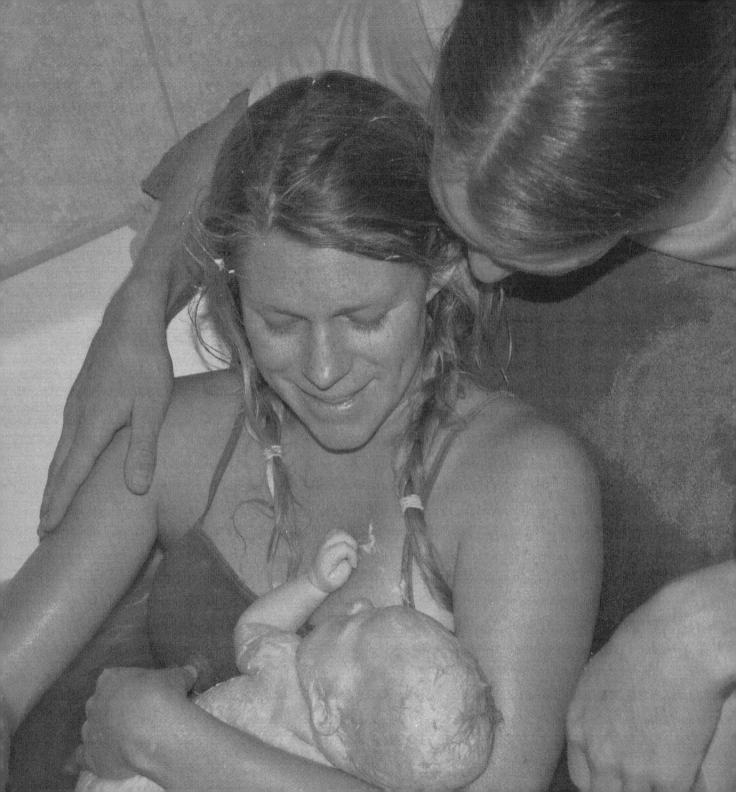

it's a new kind
of normal. a
mama-normal.

I gave birth in less than 4 hours, unmedicated, and in the birth tub at a small birth center. Due to complications, I had to push the baby out very quickly, so I tore in several places. At the time, It didn't matter to me, because I was high on birth hormones. I felt like a goddess! We found out that a baby girl had been growing inside of me, and we fell so in love.

We brought her home that night and we all slept peacefully in our bed. The next day, after failing to nurse several times, I began to worry. Wasn't she supposed to know how to nurse? Was she going hungry? I was discouraged and scared. I was also beginning to feel the physical pain that I was about to endure for many weeks to come. My entire body ached, I was bleeding heavily, and doing anything other than sleeping hurt. Our birth assistant came to do the 24 hour checkup, and tried to help with nursing. After many attempts, she determined that my nipples were not large enough for my baby's liking. She suggested I try a nipple shield. So we got a nipple shield, and I finally was able to nurse my baby. I was so relieved!

The shield complicated things, but I was happy to just be nursing. On her 2 week check up, we found out she hadn't gained any weight. I was devastated once more. I felt like I had been unknowingly starving her and like our nursing relationship would have to end. I was also struggling with the healing of my wounds, and my body felt weaker than it ever had. I had to take sitz baths twice a day and my wounds still felt raw! I was a wreck!

I had many meltdowns, but 95% them involved me, and my issues. My baby was such a calm and peaceful baby, and I didn't even appreciate it because I was too busy focusing on me! I felt like I would never have a normal functioning or looking vagina again, my body would always be weak, and that I would be a failure if my nursing relationship couldn't last. But the amazing thing is, that months down the road, you look back and see that that life happily goes on.

Things get better, and the things you once shed so many tears for, are no longer a big deal. Things go back to normal, but it's a new kind of normal. A mama-normal. You learn to go easy on your postpartum body, and if you can nurse, that's wonderful! But if you have to be a pumper or do formula, that's okay too! You learn that your vagina will heal. And if it looks a little different, it's okay because it's a product of bringing your precious baby earthside. But most importantly, you learn that being a mama is so much more than the few things you focus on in the beginning. It is forever a learning experience and your role constantly evolves. You'll always be a mama now. It is embedded in you. And just know that your baby will love you, regardless of how the little things fall into place along the way

There was a wave that washed over me when I became a mother. It gently held me within a protectively tranquil body of water. Thoughts rushed rapidly through me. I feared the unknown, and I prepared for the marathon that my body was about to run. When birth came and passed, a new flood swept me off of my feet. I was mesmerized by the surreal incredulity of becoming a mother.

My first words to my daughter were, "Are you okay?"

I did not believe that she was until the moment when I first saw her in the flesh. Sleepy, swollen eyes, soft tufts of red-blonde hair peeking out from a bloodstained hospital cap.

Each time I nursed her to sleep, I would ask her again, "Are you okay?"

I still wanted to be sure that she was. I wanted to reassure myself that she was real, and that she belonged to me. I wanted to be sure that she felt that she had made the right decision in choosing me.

I fell more deeply in love with her each day. I was intoxicated by the pool of my newfound motherhood. I didn't feel that I was swimming, nor gasping for air, but floating. Still, it was all too dream-like. All too much like water slipping through my fingertips, when all I wanted was something hard to grab hold of.

I remember those late hours, illuminated only by the dim glow of a night light in the bathroom hallway. My c-section scar ached underneath its bandage each time I shifted to coax my daughter's impossibly small body back to sleep. Scared that she would disappear if I closed my eyes, I watched her. Always smiling in her sleep and curling her fist with her thumb between her index and middle finger like she was trying to communicate with me. Trying to show me a family sign. Trying to tell me that she was okay.

I wanted to give my daughter the best start I possibly could, so every three hours I pumped. I pumped and pumped and pumped until I cried, until I was depressed, until I was exhausted. I wish that my now-self told my then-self to heed the midwive's advice.

"You don't love your baby with your breast," they said, "you love your baby with your heart. You feed a baby with food." After pumping relentlessly and trying to attach a screaming baby to my breast over and over, at exactly 4 weeks and 1 day after she was born, my daughter decided that she may as well give my milk a go, and hasn't looked back since. I yearn for this first month again. I wish I had it over and had just spent time with my daughter cuddling and bonding with her. Sometimes things don't go to plan. Motherhood teaches you to let it go.

The first few months feel as though they're never ending at times, sometimes it felt like I wouldn't make it through, and that I'd lose my mind. At times I did. Sometimes, I still do. I'm not ready to have another little bundle – I'm not sure if I ever will be. But I do know that every single moment with my daughter has enriched my life with meaning, with purpose and with banana and yogurt smears on all of my clothes. I love her.

with the birth
of my daughter,
I felt reborn.

"Mama", "Mum", "Mommy." Universal terms that once represented a global sisterhood comprised of women from different cultures and backgrounds; a community spanning generations. Nowadays, though, motherhood has too often been reduced to a competition. Breastmilk vs. formula, medicated vs. unmedicated birth, to vaccinate or not to vaccinate. Everywhere we turn, there's an article or blog post to "guide" us to becoming perfect mothers; so many voices calling us to a dance that promises fulfillment and admiration if we get every step just right.

For as long as I can remember, I have been a planner, a perfectionist, and a people pleaser. During my pregnancy, the same was true of me. I read every article and every blog to know how to achieve approval in certain mothering circles. At the time, I just convinced myself that this is what it takes to be a "good Mom."

I spent hours of my pregnancy researching everything. Safe sleep, car seats, you name it. My birth plan was short, simple, and in my mind "perfect." Then came labor day. My water broke before the sun rose and excitement set in as it would finally be the day to meet our daughter. Then, labor didn't progress. 14 hours in and countless laps around the maternity wing, yet my body wouldn't cooperate. Then came the Pitocin. I could practically hear the mommies that I had strived to please and be accepted by let out a collective gasp. The pain intensified, but I labored on. 28 hours in. Despite my best efforts, there was little progress. It came down to a decision. Accept the epidural, and hope that it would help baby girl to come out, or accept the epidural, and prepare for a c-section. Little one was born not long after the epidural; healthy and perfect to us.

As grateful as I was for a healthy baby, I felt shame though. I didn't dare share my birth story with the other mommies. When I did share with one of them, I was met with a disappointed "oh". In her mind, I knew I had "failed".

Eight months later, I no longer feel shame. I believe that I made the best decision for my daughter and myself. My daughter has already taught me some important lessons since she's been earthside. I cannot control everything around me, but I can choose to make the best of every challenge. I cannot please everyone, but the people who love me most, the people whose opinions really matter, love me without condition. With the birth of my daughter, I felt reborn-I don't need everyone's approval; I will make the decisions that are the best for ME and MY family.

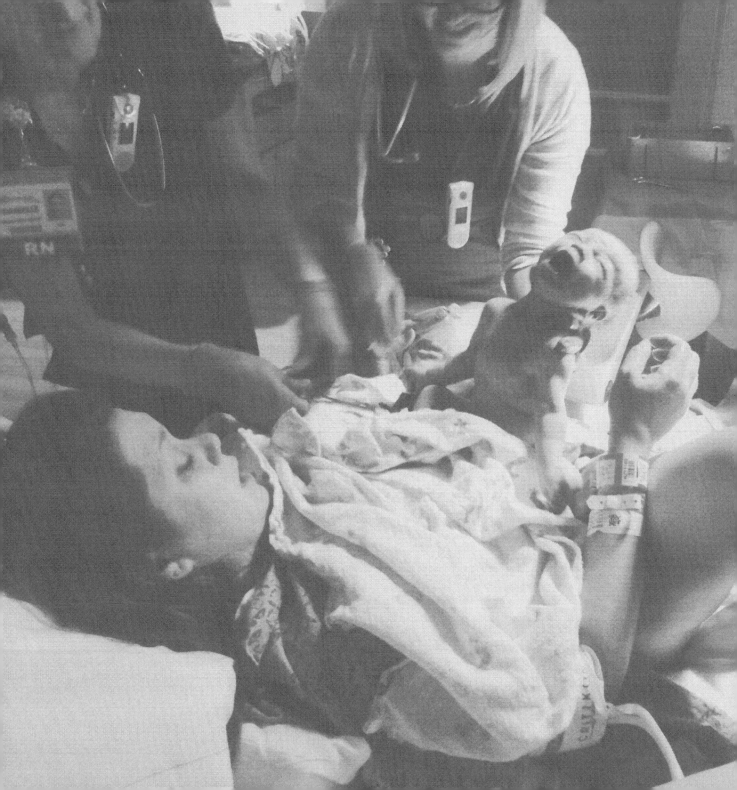

"This is so hard. It hurts. I don't know if I can do this." I remember saying these words as I helplessly clung onto the arm of my son's father, sinking my nails deeper into his flesh, while I brought our baby earth side. But I did it. And I did it scared. Much like breastfeeding. I remember those same words leaving my lips. "This is so hard. It hurts so much. I don't know if I can do this." But I did that, too. And I did it scared, for the past six months and counting. But then came the dark and heavy cloud right around the two month mark of my postpartum period.

This was my first baby, and I had no idea just how common postpartum depression and anxiety were, regardless of the fact that I now faintly remember seeing more pamphlets than I would ever really care to count every time I sat,waiting in my OB's office. But there it was. It loomed and it lingered and when it hit, it hit hard. And I thought again, "This is so hard. It hurts so much. I don't know if I can do this."

Much like everyone throughout some point during their postpartum period, I struggled. And no matter how many other mothers I spoke with, or no matter how many mom blogs I read, I still felt alone – completely isolated. Sure, there were other people, other mothers, out there who were going through what I was going through, or something similar, but in no way did being aware of any of that have any affect or influence on changing the fact that this was still my reality. I was living this day-to-day. I was struggling. And frankly, I still am.

I was embarrassed. Ashamed, really, to admit that I was suffering. So I did it, silently. And that only made it that much harder for me. My attempt to bury the darkness, to push it away and suppress the notion of feeling not only completely and utterly helpless, but insane as well, only caused me to become that much more scared. I knew that some mothers experienced periods of sadness, but to this extreme?

I was having visions of accidentally suffocating my baby while we co-slept or while he nursed, or tumbling down the concrete steps of our apartment building with him in my arms. I would imagine seeing blood everywhere every time my feet met the pavement outside our front door, leading up to those steps. I'd imagine we'd both be laying down at the bottom of those stairs, unconscious, alone, and helpless. Even just the thought of driving or being in a car terrified me. I'd see a semi-truck pass us by on the opposite side of the road and suddenly I'm lost in a trance, imagining that the truck is making a beeline for our car, head-on, and I wince. I wince at the thought of the truck crashing into us. Injuring us, or even worse, killing us both.

The delusional thoughts didn't just end there. Managing my relationships, especially the one with my son's father, began to feel much more difficult than I remembered and suddenly I was having visions of slamming fists into my partner's skull while he peacefully slept. Why? Maybe because I had a baby sucking on my nipple for the umpteenth time in a single night, while he pinched my chest with one hand and pulled ungodly amounts of hair from my head with the other, which often left me wondering when I'd actually go bald between that and the postpartum hair loss, is why.

But there had to be more to it. I had no idea I was capable of feeling that much rage or hate, especially towards the person I was so incredibly and deeply in love with. Why was I so angry? Why was I imaging these things? Was it the sleep deprivation? Or am I really just this crazy? There was so many questions that went unanswered for so long because I simply could not talk about these things. I just thought I'd be seen as an unfit mother.

Over time, it got better. By the time my son hit four or five months, his personality was starting shine through. He was developing into his own person which made our interactions a little more enjoyable and our periods of bonding a whole lot easier. "Better" didn't necessarily mean I was 100%, but the fact that my son could now smile and laugh and show affection other than just farting, puking, and drooling on me, made those dark periods much more manageable whenever they surfaced.

The day I realized that I didn't ruin my life, no matter how unrecognizable it may have seemed, was the day I decided that it didn't matter how I handled this period of time. Because I was handling it in the best way I possibly could. It wasn't about finding a magical solution or a quick fix to make it all "better." It was about figuring out how I was going to handle it, and how I was going to survive it. It was about realizing I would eventually come out stronger, and so much more resilient in the end. For myself and for my son. In no way did this define me as a person, or as a mother especially. It will, however, always be a guide, leading me along the way, helping me to navigate throughout my journey into motherhood.

Looking back, I now know that internalizing everything, instead of talking about it to death to anyone who would listen, only turned it all into depression and the depression left me angry, sad, scared, confused, isolated, and mortified. The one thing I wanted to be in life, a mother, was turning me into a monster. Or at least, it felt that way. And for that, I hated myself. I had a great pregnancy, an uncomplicated birth, a supportive partner, and a perfectly healthy and precious little baby. So, what was wrong with me?

I can't sit here and tell you that I've found the answer to that. In fact, I don't believe there is anything "wrong" with me. Contrary to popular belief, all those things I was thinking and feeling were quite normal. We just don't allow women to talk about these things. Why? And for what reason(s)? Just recently I read an article about a mother who took her own life because she was so consumed by her PPD. Why does our society have the tendency to glorify our pregnancies and postpartum periods where really everyone is mostly concerned about the baby, only? We can all see that the baby is fine and cute and squishy and yes, that's all fine and dandy, but that mother may very well be suffering. That mother who's soul has been torn in two. She has been reborn. She is broken, and matted, and scarred.

But that mother is a goddess. A goddess who needs her village. Because at some point, I can almost guarantee that there will come a time where she is thinking to herself, "This is so hard. It hurts so much. I don't know if I can do this."

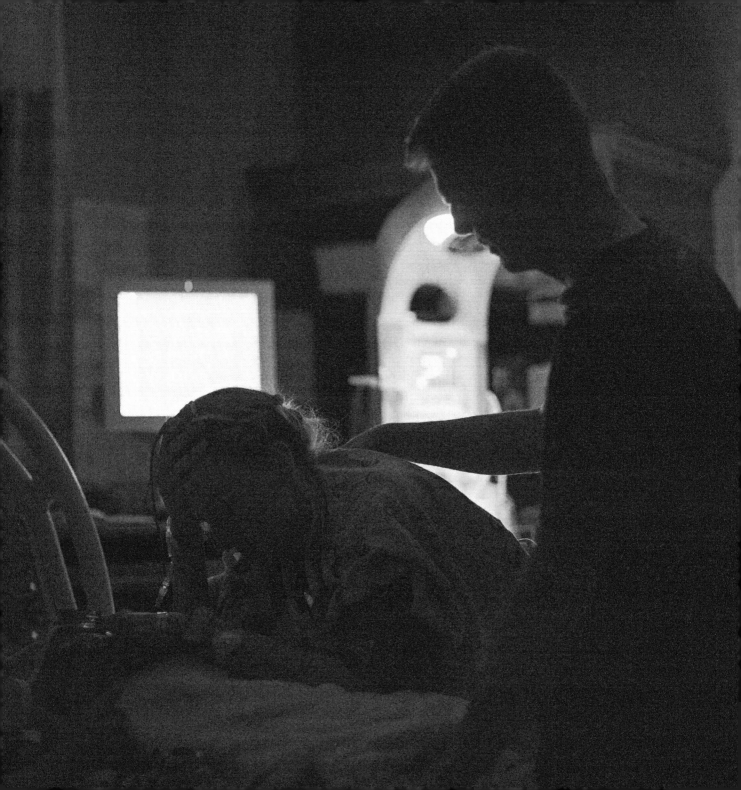

I hold her in
my heavy arms
and cry

I wear my mother's anger like a winter coat. She bundled me in it, somehow, when I was rather young. I like to think that it grew too heavy for her to carry on her shoulders alone, so she simply had to cut a piece off and sew it onto me. I'm thankful, I guess. If she hadn't shed at least a little, she might have crippled under the weight of it.

But now, here it is. Inherited fury. Borrowed rage. A woolen, stinking thing, fuzzing up my vision during the sleepless, tear-stained nights spent tending to the screams of my newborn babe. I love my daughter dearly, as my mother loved me, but at two and three and four in the morning, when all the world is dark save for my little bedroom light cutting a yellow square into the inky street, I allow my mother's anger to make me itch, and sweat, and shake.

I want to rock Aspen's bassinet over and over and over again until she stops crying. I want to give her wailing body to someone, anyone, for just a minute so that I can have a solid inhale and exhale without the sound of screams pooling in my skull. I hold her in my heavy arms and cry, and feel embarrassed that she's watching my cry, and accuse her of a million impossible things. My husband wakes to me asking the baby why she hates me, why she wants me to die, why she won't let me sleep.

Anger is, by far, the ugliest of emotions. It turns the mind black, the stomach sour, the heart cold. There is never a time when it's needed. Not ever, not once. It never helps. Anger is only kindled, never relieved. Only passed on, like draping the winter coat around another's shoulders, causing them to itch, and sweat, and shake, too.

I don't want Aspen to inherit my anger. I don't want to unknowingly sew some of it to her, especially to this silky soft baby skin before me. And so, I've learned quickly to pause. To remember, and say aloud: What does my daughter need, right now?

Maybe a diaper change. Or to be held. Or to be left alone. Or to be close to my breast. Maybe nothing at all. Sometimes, I don't know what she needs, and I'll never know. But I can be sure that the one thing she absolutely doesn't need is anger. Not now, not ever.

Knowing that, I calm. I can pick away at the fibers of my mother's anger. I can slowly, surely, happily remove the weight of this winter coat without ever having to loan some of it to Aspen.

My son made a fierce, long awaited entrance into the world on January 6th, 2015. I labored for just over 37 hours, pushing for 8 hours to birth him, only to have it end in a c-section. That was the day I met the love of my life, and in some ways, met myself, too. But, I'd be lying if I said it was an easy road after that. Emmett was absolutely, one hundred percent worth the long labor and painful recovery, but I had so much heartache over not feeling adequate, right from the start. I felt as though I had failed at birthing him and was therefore set up to fail at motherhood. I felt like a failure every time I grimaced from the pain of my incision. I felt like a failure when my baby cried and I couldn't get out of bed and pick him up due to the pain. I felt like a failure when he would cry after a feeding because I wasn't producing enough.

Throughout this journey, I've learned to bear my scar with pride and not let discouragement plague me anymore. My baby loves me, knows me and is comforted by me and that is worth more than gold. He doesn't see a failure, he sees a strong mama. I'm in the process of learning to see myself through my babe's eyes. I still have days, but I'm learning to be as patient with my heart as he is.

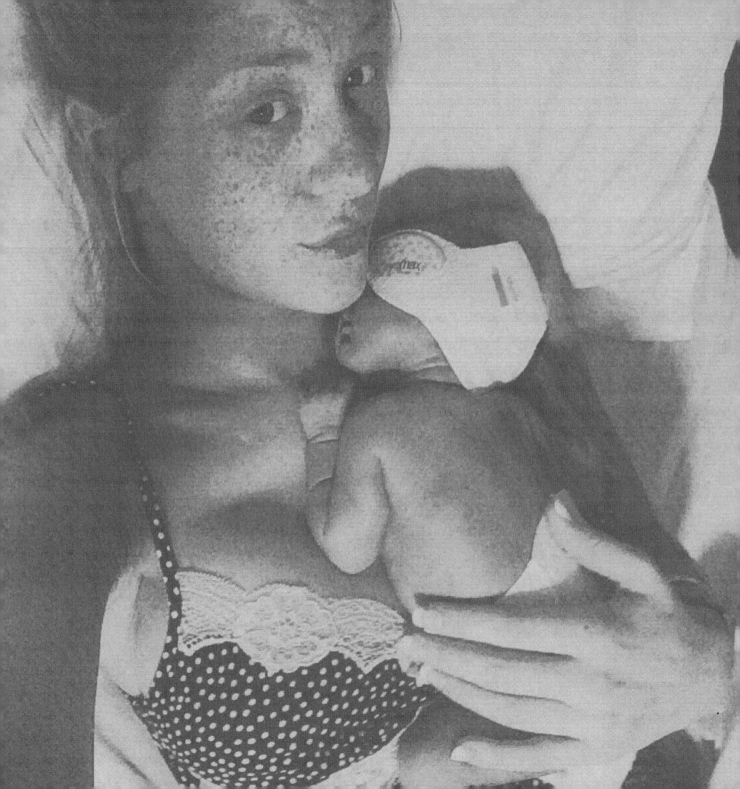

and just think,
she looked
at you first.

You held her only moments after she had breathed her very first tiny breath; the first of a million. Of a million million. She opened her eyes and calmly knew you. So tiny, she's supposed to still be tucked away in a different world. It was you who held her in the calm first.

Her next days after that were filled with needles and syringes, lying naked in baking plastic boxes, struggling with felt eye masks and borrowing hospital knitted cardigans. My dad said I looked grey when he picked us up a week later. Grey.

And the next day you were gone.

It was you she first looked at; you who held her in that oversized towelling shield. I was grey, and lost and clueless. And you still went. The first two months you were back and forth like that. Never really present when you were here. You still refuse to give yourself to her. To us. We are homeless. And you will not start working at something which will give her everything.

I am crippled both physically with arthritis and mentally with anxiety and still, you do nothing. Your mother looked me in the face and told me, so calmly, that you care more for your music than you do for me. She knew those words would pierce me like daggers. And I could feel my little one squirming at my ribs as they escaped her mouth and slapped me in the face. And I now believe her. And yet, I can't understand how you can care more about a band who have never given you a penny, who have never cared about you or your family, who are preventing you from starting a life with us; and you care about that, them, more than her. The only thing that matters. The reason I sacrificed my body and my mind; the reason I stay up staring and crying just at the beauty of her face, the thing that is so perfect I can not even put into words.

Your music. Means more. Than her.

I often fantasize when we are lying next to each other at night, together, yet so separate, house, and a sweet bedroom for her, all white with pink covers and fairy lights and fluffy rugs and vintage photo frames. Of holidays to the sea, and days out to the zoo, and on boats and cooking outside late in summer when it's still cold but we are wearing fleeces and gilets and smiles.

And I wonder why I have stayed. And I'll tell you why. Because if I leave, in some wild attempt at a better life for her, she will be a dog toy, being pulled back and forth. She will be in limbo. I won't see her every morning and that thought turns my stomach rotten. Your mother. The woman who puts herself before her own children, who's house is carpeted with Labrador hair, who spends money on furniture rather than her babies; your mother will have to look after her. My baby. Who I want everything for. I stay with you because the thought of losing her to your mother is worse. And I will deal with you leaving.

I would do anything for her. And even through all of this, your eyes still tell me that you will make it right. Behind that vacant pain, the boy who took me to the top of the world to lie on the ground and watch the sun go down until our backs were damp from cold grass, he is still there. Some day. I trust you will make it right. Someday.

And just think, she looked at you first.

Indi helped me
to find me, in
the messiest way
possible

When I got pregnant with my oldest daughter, Indi, I was young and all but homeless. The months leading up to me finding out I was in fact pregnant were spent on my bother's apartment floor after losing my job in Santa Cruz. I had a small basket of personal items, and often times didn't even have enough food to feed myself. This was a pretty accurate description of the years leading up to me becoming a mother, honestly. I was young and had been alone for years. The "fend for yourself" mentality wasn't my strong suit. I had little to no stable support or comfort outside of my sister's nurturing nature when she could afford it. During this time, I had started a brief affair with the biological father of my first two children. He was older, and suffered from severe emotional issues. This led me to move to back Washington state - the first time since I had left it when I was 16 - in hopes of starting over and going to school to study Art History and seek a wholeness in life that was robbed from me in my childhood. I got off the plane in Seattle, sick to my stomach yet starving. It was in a Target bathroom, at age 18, that I found out I was going to be a mother. I was not ready.

I preface this because I feel like it's telling of the progression, of the pains and the transformation that motherhood has taken in my life. After I had found out I was expecting, I was fortunate enough to find employment at a local insurance agency as a secretary. I had a giant baby shower thrown for me in which I was provided everything you could imagine you would need (and not need), and I was living in an apartment with her biological father - hoping for a miracle that we would be a family in the most classic of senses. I felt as though these physical steps towards what I saw as "preparedness" or "stability" in the classic terms were enough to get me started as a mother.

During labor, I was not only induced, but opted for an epidural and was diagnosed with pre-eclampsia. It was traumatic, and not in the slightest bit romantic or empowering. When I brought her home, I cried for hours out of fear of not knowing what to do. I was terrified that I had just done this baby lamb of a human a disservice by being her mother. During first month I had all but failed at breastfeeding, being told by my then mother-in-law that she was starving and needed formula. I had held tight to my values as a vegan, vegetarian to which I was told my breast milk probably wasn't adequate enough to satisfy her. This was an emotional blow for me, but not as much as knowing that I had the responsibility of motherhood - something my own mother failed at in epic proportions. It triggered every past memory of emotional abuse, while solidifying the importance of the job I had been given, the impact of motherhood. It wasn't until a month in, a month of chaos trying to figure out how to feed, change and sleep this little human - who all but felt like a stranger - that I saw her. Like, really saw her.

I saw her soul, her beauty, her incredible specialness - all behind her big brown eyes. My relationship with Indi is special, because in that one month that I completely lost myself both physically and emotionally, it was in that same month that I found my heart.

Motherhood didn't come naturally to me in the way you'd imagine it to, and I guess that makes sense since, I never really saw it demonstrated naturally. I needed to connect and learn, truthfully, to the human that came through me - the human that was entirely individually her own person. I can't pretend to take credit for who she is now. She was born with her own soul and mind, and just like falling in love, there are bumps, growths, and periods of truth that only brings you more centered into yourself. Indi helped me find me, in the messiest way possible, and I intend to do the same for her.

Now a mother of three daughters, I credit this learning curve, this painful experience of self awareness, as my guiding light. I am raising women, and I want them to know their humanity as well as their value individually. Through my rough entrance into motherhood I learned that its their individuality that makes them so special, and makes mothering them so rewarding.

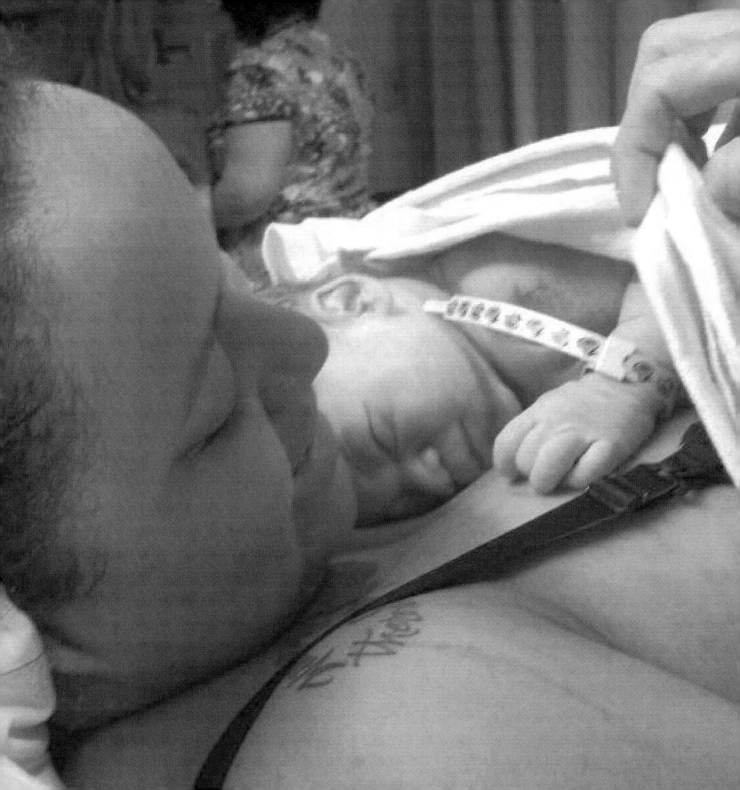

I could feel myself transitioning from a girl, to a mother

Becoming a mother was absolutely nothing I could have prepared myself for. I spent nearly 10 months envisioning myself, makeup on, hair done, body back to normal, with a cooing, smiling baby in my arms.

Sure, every other mother told me that I'll be exhausted. That I'll rarely find time to shower or to eat. That it's the hardest, but also the best job in the world to be a mother. I would just smile and nod.

Then, I gave birth to my son and realized the one thing no one warned me about; the range of emotions being a mother would fill my soul with. How the amount of pride and love and wonder you feel when you first see the little human you've created can easily match the feelings of loss you feel for your previous life.

Suddenly I had this eight pound, screaming, cluster nursing little boy to take care of while simultaneously trying to take care of my bleeding, broken, sewn up postpartum body. Just remembering to eat was a chore. I was, and still am, the only one that could soothe him to sleep or get him to stop crying. Why? Because I had the boobs. I had to be there for him, for my husband's sanity, for everyone's sanity. I was an on-call milk machine and I resented my body for that. But worse, I resented my baby for that.

I craved a minute alone. Or a nap that didn't end 10 minutes later with screams. Every quick shower I was able to steal, I cried through. I cried while he cried, I cried when he wouldn't let me out him down to shovel a bowl of cereal down my throat. I just cried. I could physically feel myself transitioning from a selfish, know-it-all girl, to a humbled, constantly learning, protective mother. I was a mother. Not the Hallmark card version that we're all told to be, but a mother of my own definition.

The funny thing is, as soon as I was away from him, I felt like a bad mom. My stomach would churn with the idea that he needed me and I wasn't there for him. But it was more so that I needed him. I spend 98% of my day with this small person and have learned so much about him. What he likes, what makes him burp the best, what makes him fall asleep the fastest. He was my little man, and my heart ached to see his little face again. To see him looking back at me with those curious eyes. Even to smell his spit up breath when I tried to kiss his little lips. I missed him.

He's three weeks old today and I'm just now getting a schedule down with him. Every new thing he does makes my heart fall to pieces with joy and pride. I know I have so much more to learn with this little firecracker, but with this new skin I wear, I'm so overwhelmingly excited about it all.

"First and last," I repeat to myself as I sit trying to pee in my three day old daughter's bathtub filled with lukewarm water, rosemary, and chamomile. This is the only way that I can, since I'm stuck in bed recovering from a postpartum hemorrhage, faint, flushed, and feeling the affects of the "hormone crash." My daughter is always sound asleep beside me while I struggle for thirty minutes preparing myself to go to the bathroom. It is almost like she knows waking up would be too much of a strain on me physically, emotionally, and mentally, so she continues to sleep until after the process is over and my husband and best friend are able to lift me up out of the tub, place me onto a new bed pad, as I regain my strength.

I didn't know it was possible to have a postpartum hemorrhage or that some women had a hard time breastfeeding due to a low milk supply because of it. I didn't know that breastfeeding would hurt: it hurts so badly it brings me to tears, I kick my husband, squeeze his hand, and hit myself as I try to ignore the discomfort involved in feeding my baby naturally. Breastfeeding looks so beautiful, peaceful, and harmless in all the photographs I have seen of women striving to normalize it and bond with their child, but no one talks about how painful it is. No one talks about how my nipples would be pulled and stretched out over a matter of days, throbbing, bloody, scabbed, and sore. Everyone is too busy arguing about formula versus breast milk to mention what it really is like and that breastfeeding is something mom and baby have to learn.

I knew that in meeting my child I would experience a love I had never known, a love that only parents can feel, one so deep and profound it swells your heart and makes you cry. And I knew that in an instant my child would become my new favorite person. However, I didn't know my favorite person could make me question having a child or that someone who fills my days with light would also fill them with darkness. I didn't know that she would make me question the appointment I canceled eight months prior after deciding that having a baby would be my greatest adventure.

Six weeks. The time frame that every woman is held to, whether they know it or not. The supposed marker for success in being a great Lover, and wife. 6 weeks. It's crap. Well, for me, it was. I mean, who typifies the so-called "norm" these days, anyway?

So, here is my raw truth; The hormones that ravaged my body were so foreign; so innate, but so unknown. They were never a part of how I learned to cope with intimacy, and love, and being a whole human being. I was lost. Postpartum. Feeling a mess. Trying to manage the rapid tear-fall at the earth-shaking glory of that fresh-skinned human I just made.

I just carried. I just birthed. I just named. Feeling powerful and yet so utterly small and full of fear. Because if I lost this soul, what could the world ever hold of beauty again, right? How shattering is this love? That from one moment to the next is terrifying only because of the fear that the next rise and fall of that sweet chest won't take place on cue. And, those crazy-big-love-feelings didn't go away when I was being intimate. The struggle to engage my brain in any other way seemed futile. I simply wasn't ready. And, that wasn't because I wasn't madly, deeply, soulfully, crazy in love with my Lover. Loving him through this journey was magic in itself. The way he looked at me when I was in the throes of labor was like reading words on his face that I didn't know he could articulate; the fear on his face that he also needed everything to be okay and that he felt so small in the midst of it, and then the broken look on his face when he saw me mourning the loss of that elusive vaginal delivery as I was prepped and whisked away for an emergency c-section.

I love him to the core of who I am. I love him deeper than I ever knew how to. But. That love was so pure. So full of magic. So much about being a mother - this ground-pulsing, monstrously spiritual and emotional transformation. And, the act of sex seemed somehow misplaced in the midst of those enormous feelings. It was silly, really - I knew that in my mind. But it felt inappropriate to my brain.

I thought, "Dude, I'm a MOTHER. A mother! I mean, I can't be having sex and stuff."

I felt crazy. For weeks I held onto those glorious 6 weeks that I knew my husband was prepared for. Prepared to wait for my body to heal. To be ready for intimacy. I almost felt guilty, because I hadn't delivered my son vaginally, so did I still deserve a 6 week reprieve from sexual intimacy? And, then. The infamous 6th week ended. I gave in because of love. I could read his desire in the way he touched me on the shoulder as I rocked my son to sleep. As he grazed my bare leg in bed when I was surveying my changed bodily form. I knew he wanted me.

So, that glorious 6 week mark, huh? Crap. Pure crap. It didn't work. I was swollen; dry and parched and empty. The burning from our attempt lasted days later, and I nearly sobbed myself to sleep. Because I ached for my husband. For the truths I wasn't telling him. That I just wasn't ready yet. Before long, it became clear that I must be vastly abnormal, right? (At least, this is what I'd been programmed to believe). That something must really be wrong here. That we would probably never be able to be intimate again!

I made an appointment with my Midwife, and tearfully told her my story. She told me that I was normal, that 6 weeks was an arbitrary number, and that she could prescribe me something to help, but that it would probably limit my breast milk supply. That just wasn't even an option. My husband would just have to wait. My baby needed me. For sustenance. Nourishment. Skin on skin time. He didn't bat an eye. He knew. And, he waited. It wasn't until 6 months after my son was delivered, that we "successfully" engaged in sex. I was still so very sore afterwards, but it worked.

In the end, the journey taught me what it was like to be a parent in a marriage. Finding ways to connect the soul, the body, the brain, in a million other ways. I remember one night after a failed attempt, I had burrowed into a ball in our bed with my hands over my face. Ashamed I couldn't be there for him, for his needs. That I felt selfish that I wasn't all that unhappy about it. That I couldn't turn off the new "voices" in my head - these conflicting mother-voices. The ones that worried if my son woke up, I couldn't get to him right away. That it would be awkward to nurse him immediately after being intimate with my husband.

And, then everything melted away. We talked. We got real. Instead of disappointment, he listed all of the ways he found me even more lovely than before as he traced his fingers along my new, naked, wrinkled, flabby, saggy body. We listened to our favorite record (an old Sigur Ros album) and lay together sharing warmth for what felt like days. It was healing. It lifted my guilt, and that is what ultimately made the difference, in my brain. It allowed me to loosen up, to lay myself bare. My emotions, my personal revelations, my worries, my fears, my intense joys. The ways that this new body felt to me, what I felt I lost, where I felt most raw and insecure. I had to engage my brain and force myself to recognize the woman in the mirror.

I had to learn myself all over again. What made my senses soar. What made me weak in the knees. It was all about my engagement with my own body, and being okay to wait until my body was ready. So - throw away the time-lines. Whether it be 6 weeks, or a few days. Find ways to love your new skin, for that new budding woman within so powerful and lovely.

Tonight I feel like a woman who wants everything. Who wants her back rubbed and her feet up against the edge of the couch. I want a shower and something warm and creamy to drink and to breathe slowly for the first time all day. I want to light up a cigarette and stand outside, not because I smoke or because I fancy starting, but because I've always been envious of those little breaks smokers have spattered about their day. I want to lay on the floor until someone picks me up and puts me to bed.

I want him to see that I'm working hard, that I'm doing the best that I can, that there are things I do that he doesn't see, like folding his socks into neat little bundles, and wiping down the inside of the butter tray, and scraping the dried toothpaste from the sink. Tonight, I don't want him to touch me. Not because I don't love him, but because I've had too many sticky milk curdled hands against my breasts and my face and my arms since before the sun rose this morning. Tonight, I am a woman who wants everything and nothing, all at once.

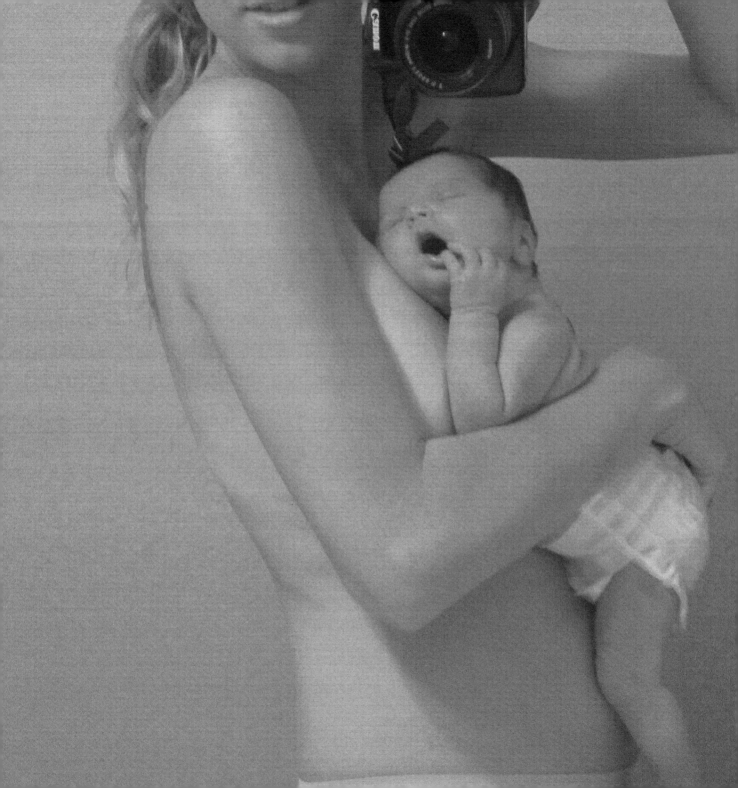

as she took her
first breath,
I took mine.

As she took her first breath, I took mine. Her sweet cries filled me, I was given life through her birth. I knew I was broken, I knew I needed saving, but I never dreamed that I would be made whole through her. In one instant the strength I had been searching my whole life for was in my arms, latched on to my breast and we fed each other exactly what we both needed in that moment.

Looking back, I see myself pregnant with my baby bee. I had twinges of the strength I was also pregnant with. I said I was keeping her, she was mine. I refused to name her "Rose" or "Grace." She had a name in my heart long before she was in my womb. I held firm that I planned to breastfeed and I returned all those bottles I received at the baby shower from those who tried to tell me I was kidding myself and that I would never succeed. I ignored those who told me the "horrors" of giving birth. And on her birthday, I chose the way she would come into this world: un-medicated, with only love surrounding her.

But this new strength, this true momma bear power I felt in that instant was like no other. I was reborn a mother. This strength became the downfall of my relationship with her biological father and the rise to finding my self-worth. I now had a reason to live. I had to be baby bee's mommy.

A name with so much meaning. Mommy is the protector, the unconditional love, the warmth, the first friend, the arms you run to. He didn't want this, not any bit of it. Not the baby. Not the responsibility. Not the love.

Because he had no love for me, or for himself. He hated seeing me stand up, be strong, powerful and demand what I knew was right for baby bee. I was breastfeeding her and wearing her. I did all the things my heart and mind said to do without interference from others, even him. I didn't need anyone but her. And I was happy. Baby bee was happy. He could see my strength shining.

I knew I had to leave. The abuse was getting worse. Verbal, a slap, objects thrown, me thrown, bruised, bleeding, strangled. Never to baby bee, only to me while she slept peacefully. I had to stay long enough for him to get caught and charged. That would protect her. He wouldn't be able to scare me with threats of taking her from me. I needed it on paper what he did. I needed a neighbor to call when they heard the yelling, the banging. And it happened. They finally came, and took him away. Just shy of her one month birthday. He can no longer deny what he did. He can no longer hurt me, or ignore her.

And it is just us, me and baby bee. Like always, strong and happy. Now we are free.

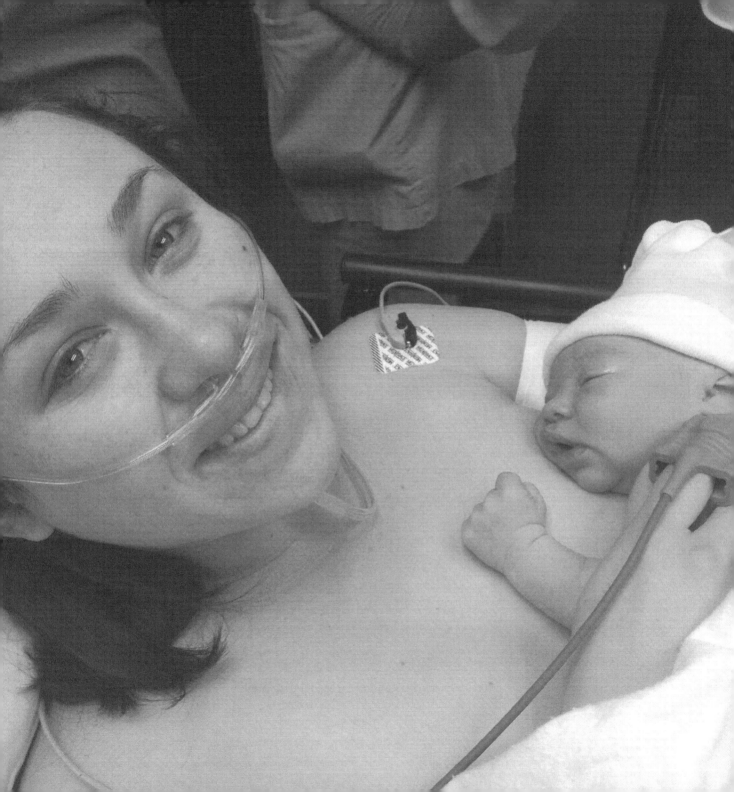

you were made
in love.
you will always
be loved.

Nothing went as planned with your birth, but it was still beautiful. As I sit here rocking you, your mouth tugs at my breast and I hear you breathe. Your little legs move and your tiny hand opens and closes on my chest. You fall asleep and milk spills from your lip and flows down my side, over the curves that carried you. This mom thing is hard. My body is different. I cry all the time and I feel so incapable. Sometimes I fear I'm unable to protect you, love you, and care for you the way you need me too. At night I pray for you and for the grace to mother you the way you need.

The first days were the hardest. I hovered over you to make sure you were still breathing. I cried because I was weak, mentally, physically, and emotionally. I cried because your daddy and I would no longer be just us. Our routine, nonexistent. We can't spend hours tangled up together. But at night, I lay you down to sleep and I crawl in bed exhausted, un-showered, covered in milk, and feeling like my cup can't be filled anymore. Your daddy reaches out for me and pulls me close. He tells me I'm the most beautiful thing in the world and that he's proud of me...that I'm an amazing mama. He says this, and I look at you, and I shatter.

You are my life. He is my life. I might fail and feel incompetent, but that doesn't mean that I am either. It means I'm human. I'm a mother and wife. I'm a nurturer and protector. I'm a lover and a helper. But most importantly, I'm still me. I'm growing, and learning, and messing up, and teaching myself. I'm me with a million times more love. I embrace my body, flaws and all, because I carried you. I embrace the spilt milk, because I know I won't always make it. I don't care if I'm messy. I'll forget a shower if it means I can stare at you for that extra 10 minutes. And your daddy and I? Our love has grown so much. Every time we look at you we fall more in love because in front of us lies proof of our incredible, indescribable love for each other. You were made in love. You will always be loved.

I promise to always try my hardest to be everything you need me to be. I will always remember these sweet moments of you curled up next to me in my big bed and the sweet little sounds that escape from your newborn body. You're so tiny and you've changed my life forever. It's hard and wild and crazy and exhausting, but I get to be your mama. I will do anything for you. You shatter me daily and it's the greatest thing in the world. I love you little Leif, my bear cub, my milky man. My son.

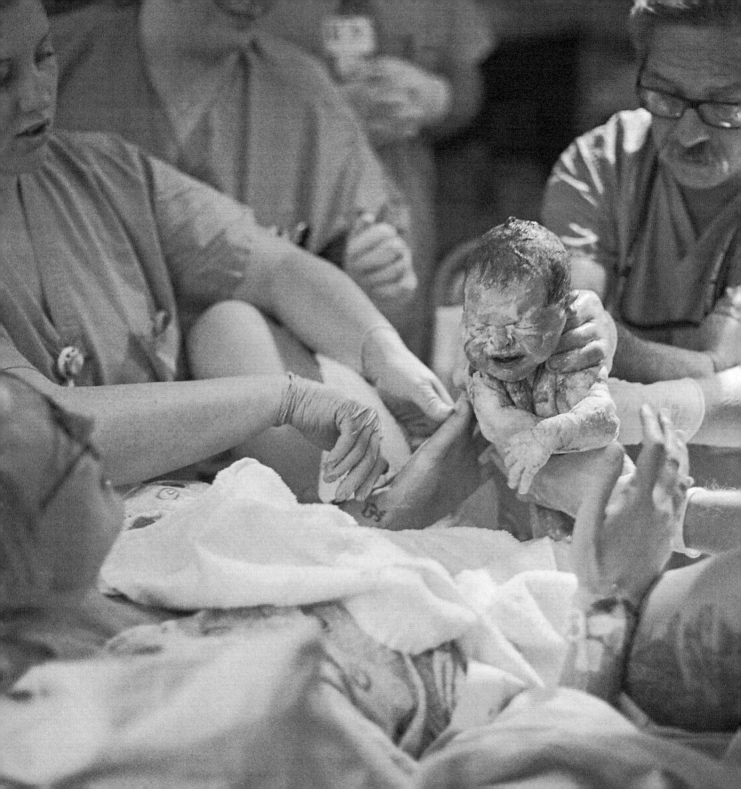

Aspen is a strange and wonderful little beastie. Trapped somewhere between the spirit world and ours, ocean eyes searching the walls, the sky, the skin on my face. Knowing nothing and everything, all at once. She is the most marvelous sort of empty. Like the desert, like the cosmos, spacious and new and old and allowing all the world to pour into her. I feel the presence of many ancient and wise beings with her in these early days, maybe guardians sent to watch over her transition from one side, to the other.

I thought that I would know her completely when she was placed on my chest at birth. Like we would be old friends. Instead, she's a wild and unfamiliar creature, all animal noises and smacking, thirsty lips. She teaches me what soothes her (steady bouncing, constant movement, cradling her fuzzy head in my palms) and I teach her how to smile, how to coo, how to sleep soundly in the crook of my arm. We're slowly learning how to handle one another. And it's a beautiful relationship, really. More than just a mother towering over her child, always right, always older. Rather, we are equal. Both children: new, learning. I hope it's always like this, even when she's as old as I am now. Her learning from me, and I from her, a friendship, sharing, growing together in love, and in life, and in Spirit.

These early weeks will be lost before long, I can tell. They're already such a blur of messy diapers and midnight milk soaked towels and bedsheets. But I don't want to forget. Not the way the apartment smells (kind of sour, kind of sweet, all covered up with lavender and incense), or the way chores that used to only take a moment (putting a fresh bag in the trash) now take minutes on end and one hand, not two. Not the way she throws her little, dinosaur arms into the air and frowns every time a noise or a touch startles her. Not the way her papa looks at her in wonder, strokes her cheek with his thumb, calls her his squid, his little bird, his love. Not the way she fall asleep like a frog on my chest. Not the way she is right here, right now, all soft and new and perfectly empty.

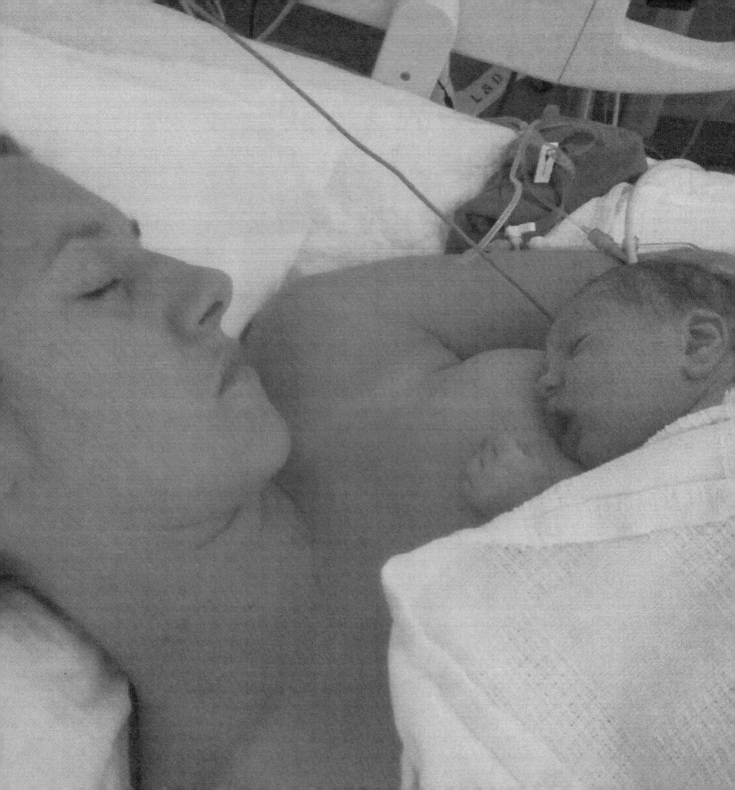

I was taken to the hospital by ambulance for an emergency cesarean. I had a low lying placenta and when labor began, so did bleeding. I was put under and did not meet my son until four hours after his birth. When the time came for me to meet him I thought, "are you sure he's mine?" He didn't look like I had pictured and I didn't feel the overwhelming love people talk about. Rather, I felt confused and scared as they held him to me so he could try nursing. I thought it was the drugs, but when we left the hospital three days later the disconnected feeling remained.

Over that first month, I would see my husband being all mushy in love over our son and I would feel guilt. "How could I, a mother, not love my baby?"

I felt guilty because I had to have a cesarean. I was not awake to hear his first cry and be the one to console him. I thought, "If I was really his mother, I would have been there for him." I had failed as a mother because I couldn't give my son the start in the world I thought he deserved (natural birth) and therefore I was no good for him. I didn't think I qualified as a mom. I didn't want to attend any mom's groups or get into conversations about birth experiences because I felt extremely inadequate. I told myself I didn't deserve to be called a mom. When I would open up, people would often respond with, "Well, at least you and baby are healthy." I did not find this helpful. I did not feel healthy, I felt traumatized. It was a very lonely time for me as I felt no one understood what I had gone through and why loosing the birth I had dreamed of was so devastating to me.

I wish I had known that some mothers are not born the instant you meet your child, but rather it is a process that can take days, weeks, months or even years. I am now over the moon and completely in awe of my son. It took a few months, but at some point, it was as if my heart broke at the realization that this sweet boy was my child. That it was him who was growing inside me all those months. I still mourn my birth experience, but I recognize that he was birthed from my body. My body went through a lot. I sometimes just cry now because I love him so much and I never knew I could love someone this deeply. I am his mother, and he is my son.

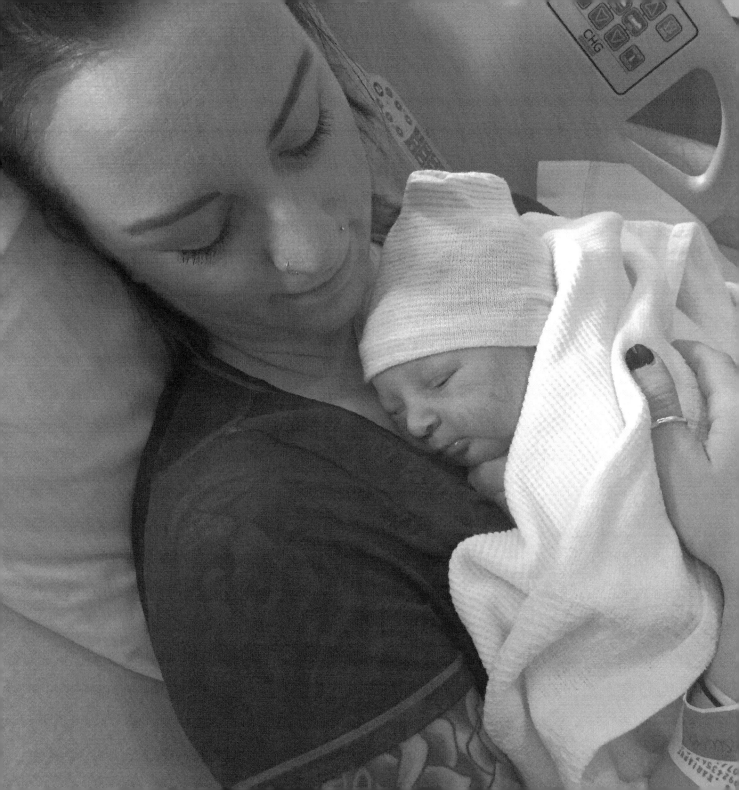

motherhood is
the most
beautiful place
I have ever
known

I remember the moment so clearly. They sat me down in a wheelchair just outside my hospital room. I was going home. We were going home. I realized I had spent 2 whole days inside that room, never once peering past the closed door. A recluse in the safe confines of my sterile nursery, I played house from a remote-controlled bed while nurses brought me pitchers of water and taught me the proper swaddle technique. But there I was, about to head out into the world, feeling like it would be for the first time. As if the birth of my daughter was somehow my own, and I would be going home to care for two new, fragile lives, instead of one. That's when it hit me - the tidal wave of raw emotions. They wheeled me down the hospital halls, and out into the unknown.

I spent the first week at home a stranger to my body. A stranger to my life. Through heavy eyes, I studied the sleeping beauty in my arms. "You are perfection, my little one. I love you so much it hurts. Yes, of course I am physically hurt. Torn apart where my body exhaled to allow you into this world. But my emotional and spiritual beings are writhing in pain."

"Baby blues," they would say. And, "It's normal."

But how had I not heard of this before? I had felt so prepared.

"Postpartum depression? No, I'm not worried about that. What could possibly make me sad during the most exciting and sought-after moment of my life?"

Now I had this beautiful, tangible piece of my soul to hold onto, and yet I mourned for my empty belly. From the comfort of my own home, my loving husband by my side, I longed for the security blanket of my hospital room and 24-hour care. I wanted to shout from the rooftops the wonders and joyous tales of my sweet daughter, yet every time I opened my mouth, I found only gut-wrenching sobs. I doubted myself as a wife, as a mother, and as a woman. I spent countless nights awake in my bed, my young one nestled close to my body to nourish her own, seeking advice. I wanted to feel normal. But more importantly, I needed to know those blues would subside.

And then it happened. This time, it was slow. Much slower. We began finding our rhythm; silently communicating our needs to one another, feeling our way through this new life together.

In celebration of her first month outside my body, I shared with her the story of her birth and breathed a healing sigh of relief as each word was spoken. I realized, in those moments, that I had been born anew, the morning my daughter took her first breath. All of the tears and bittersweet emotions were preparing me for my new journey into the world of motherhood. A place so frightening and awe-inspiring; The most beautiful place I have ever known.

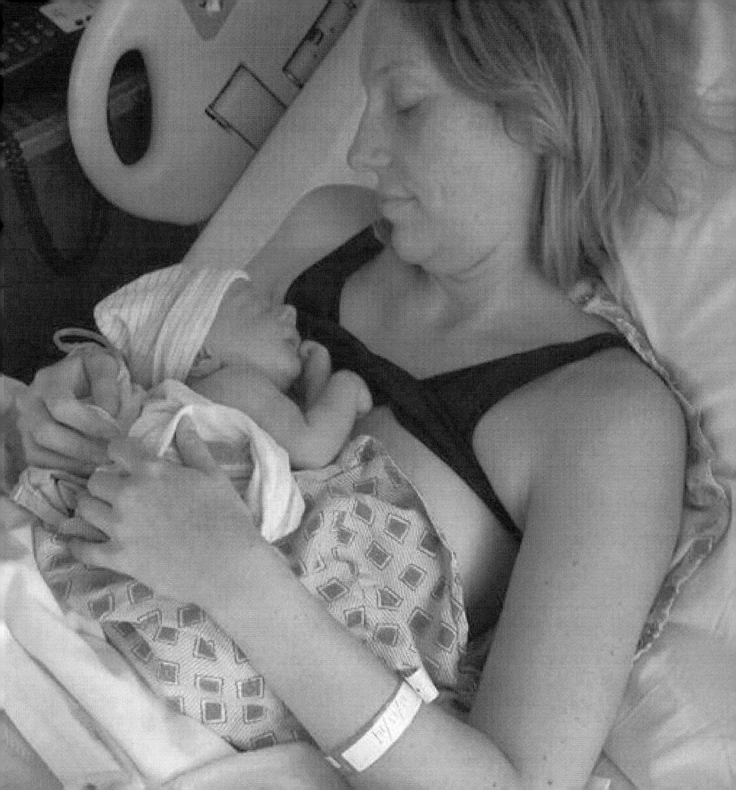

Pain. Discomfort. Soreness. Emotional breakdowns. Crying. Exhaustion. Unaccepting of new body. Of new scar. Blame it on any one of these reasons. Or all.

It wasn't him, it was me. It wasn't in one of those, "Oh, he's just saying this to get laid" types of moment. I knew he truly meant it when he said I was still beautiful. That my new body was still sexy to him. That he really missed the physical closeness more than the act. It took weeks before I felt okay to be held. We had, or I should say tried, sex at seven weeks and it felt like the first time all over again, not in a good way. I didn't understand that even with a cesarean how much I would be affected down there. I had a new body and had to learn how to use it. Once a week. That was my goal. At four months it finally felt okay, meaning it didn't make me want to cry from pain. It wasn't going to get better on its own. We needed to heal together.

Not only my son enjoyed my new, full breasts. But to me, they were only for nourishment. (Not to mention my nipples were always sore as hell.) Any other touch felt wrong. Like a violation of his territory and my new momma-space. I found myself setting boundaries: "You can touch them but no nipples," and, "You can give a soft squeeze but no massaging." He was so kind and patient. I knew he wanted more intimacy; I tried to let him know that my hesitation was not at all about my feelings toward him.

We are just hitting six months as parents. Life has changed dramatically. It's been extremely hard some days. Amazing some days. Every day it's been worth every painful second. We haven't increased how frequently we are intimate, but when we are it is comfortable and meaningful. Maybe we won't ever get back to the physical passion from pre-baby, and maybe he will get a few more head scratches, but where we are today is okay. I try to not think longingly about past times, but instead accept this new phase as life now. The passion is now formed from a deeper love and appreciation between parents. And that is as real as we can be.

My husband and I were married exactly 10 days before I got pregnant. Our year as newlyweds was stolen by a bald, round, perfect little ball of chub named James. What I envisioned for that first year was quickly replaced by trying to stay afloat during the newborn stage. Both of us sleeping in shifts: on the couch, on a chair, on the floor, on the tiny corner of our bed trying desperately not to wake the baby, anywhere we could get some sort of shut eye to keep us remotely rested.

The moment I first saw my husband holding our son, I knew he would be a great dad. A present dad, a loving dad. A dad who truly enjoys and takes pride in having the responsibility of another life. But that moment is when I realized I had to start to remind myself that he is my husband first, and our son's dad second. He is the man I chose to spend my life with, the partner to share my days with, the person who knows my ups and downs and who can make me laugh no matter what the circumstance. The person I fell in love with hard and who I made a commitment to. Having a baby brings so much joy, so much goodness and such a pure perspective on life. It solidifies a marriage into a family - a commitment so deep, it's threaded with gold.

But the foundation of that family is the relationship you have with your partner. That relationship sets the tone and leads the way. It's the first crucial example your child will have for love, respect and partnership. That's why it needs to come first. In those moments when you are overwhelmed by exhaustion and feel the urge to do the comparison game, realizing you've racked up more points in the parenting game and the resentment starts to leak in: take a minute. Take a minute to see him as you did on your wedding day. Take a minute to realize that man and woman you once were still exist. They are very much alive. Because one day, when the baby-phase-sleep-deprived-fog lifts, (and it will!), there the two of you will be, stronger and more solidified than ever before. You will see that being in the thick of the blowouts, the sleep regressions, the late night snuggle sessions and the feelings of being defeated were all essential moments needed to learn the hard lessons of parenthood. Those moments are where all the growth happens. Your new identity as "mom" and "dad" will give you a complete new meaning and understanding of each other and life, but don't lose sight of the love that brought your both together in the first place.

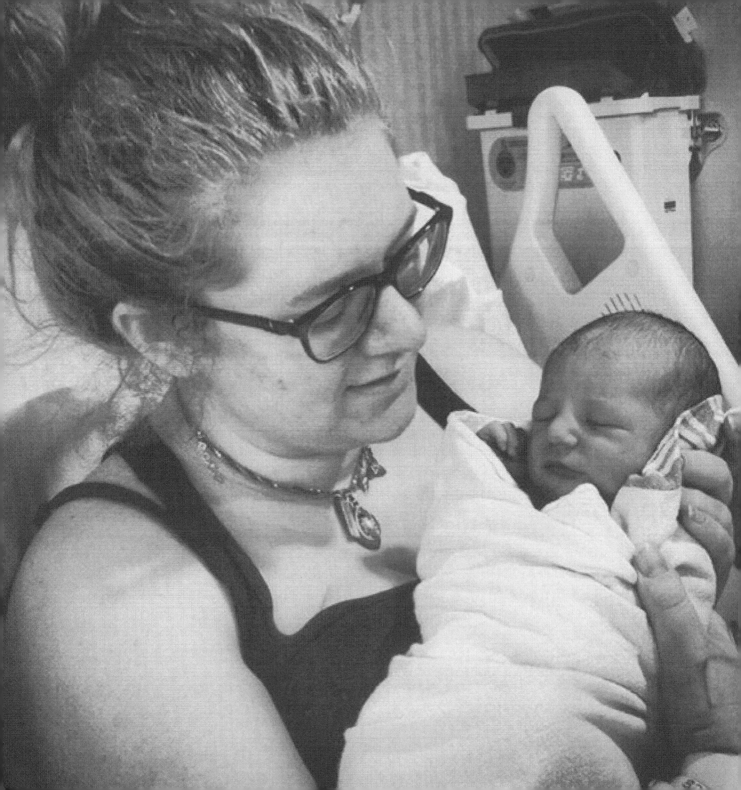

in the moment
of Willow's birth,
I became love.
I became mother.

I swear, my heart damn near exploded when they handed her to me. Seventeen months on and I'm certain my liquefied brain is still sitting in a puddle on that hospital room floor. I'd expected to be overcome with emotion the moment I laid eyes on her, but I felt nothing. I thought nothing. In that moment, I simply was. We simply were, together. As I looked down at her through a film of sweat and tears, I smiled and said, "We did it."

"No, you did it."

I remember being startled when her father spoke. I'd forgotten anyone else was in the room (or anywhere, for that matter). I didn't look up at him but I could hear the disconnection in his voice, and in that moment I knew that we were finished. I didn't let that thought occupy any real estate in my mind that night, though. That night belonged to Willow, and I wouldn't let anything take that away from her.

I didn't realize how loud the cacophony of labor and delivery and the celebration of new life was until after all the nurses and grandparents and Willow's dad finally left for the night, leaving the two of us alone in the dark and silent hospital room. Before they walked out I'd been nervous about being left on my own (I imagined calling out after them, "Excuse me! Yeah, I think there's been a misunderstanding—you see, this tiny, delicate, very breakable little person has been left in my care, but I'm just a child who happens to have very recently pushed said little person out of her vagina and who is still bleeding profusely and hasn't quite figured out how to get out of bed on her own yet. Is there maybe someone out there who would like to stay and take care of me?"), but I said nothing. The door closed behind them and I sat propped up in the hospital bed with my child in my arms and an emptiness in my Self that I've only recently been able to comprehend.

I felt guilty that I didn't experience Love for my daughter in the way I'd expected to, the way I'd felt Love for others in the past. I assumed, of course, that it would be a great and powerful Love, but that it would at its core resemble the emotion as I'd always felt it before. I was wrong. Of course, it's easy for me now to look back on that day and to describe what happened in that room with the eloquent understanding that only comes with time and deep reflection, to explain that I didn't feel Love because in the moment of Willow's birth I became Love; I became a Mother. But it took me months to even begin to recognize that truth, and I still have days when I struggle to understand it. I look back on that night and watch myself sitting there, uncertain and terrified and ecstatic and exhausted and completely alone, and I wish I could crawl in to that bed next to my Self and cradle her in my now well-trained Mother's arms, to soothe her in the way she will, with time, learn to soothe the sleeping babe in her arms.

Where did we lose it? It's only been two years, we've had our first child and here, four months later, I'm trying to make myself up for you. Reapplying deodorant, wiping my face clean from our day out in town and double checking to make sure the babe is still fast asleep . Getting sweaty palms thinking of my approach. I feel as if I'm 17 again, with my first love. You look up with innocent eyes, curious, as if I have a question for you. Pulling my shirt up, I show you the lace underwear I anxiously changed into and you grin, ear to ear.

"You don't look at me the same," I said to you, with tears in my eyes. You had that *here we go again* look on your face, and it made me want to cry even more. I could tell you didn't understand, no matter how many times I explained. You just wanted it to be quiet, you wanted your peace and so did I. Yet I was dealing with the broken heart, lost and misunderstood.

I would lie under you thinking how it wasn't fair. Sacrificing my body to satisfy your selfish need. How could you use me and think of another? It was all in my head.

I spoke to you in subtle words and spilled my heart and aches. A look of disappointment and you replied, "I thought I was making love to you, don't condemn me." I break a little more inside, and realize it is me. I am a victim of myself.

Our emotions can become truly ravishing, they take over the real world and things seem impossible. Slow down. Relax. And breathe.

it was like
falling in love
a second time.

No one ever told me how much having a baby would make me miss my husband. I ached for him all over, the way things used to be, freely loving and laying around the apartment and talking about silly, little things into the early hours of the morning. I missed him then, more than I ever had, even when he was sitting right next to me.

A part of the old me was hanging around. The one without child. The twenty-two year old spit fire, dancing long and wild into the night. Now, there I was, torn in two from the labor, clinging white-knuckled to the way things were. That wild part of me mostly slipped away when Aspen was born, and what was left of her was resisting change, even though for the most part, the change was lovely and sweet.

I missed my husband, and so for a few days in the early weeks of Aspen's life, I hated him, because he seemed like a foreign, lazy creature that sat about while I vacuumed and bled through my underwear and slung a screaming beastie over my breast for the third time in an hour. I didn't ask him to help, even though I should have. I expected him to know that I needed him. And when he didn't, my insides silently soured.

On the ninth night, he woke up to the sound of me sobbing over a child that I loved too much to put down, and I was too tired to control the words on my tongue, so I told him that I hated him, that I couldn't stand him, that I felt like a single mother. And then, I watched my husband cry for the rest of the night. I was too tired to sort through the words in my head, so we both lay there, quiet and broken and sorry, with a squirming bundle of new life snuggled up between us.

But there was relief, on day thirteen. We ate. We rested. We slept. Aspen found solace in the sound of the rain, and fell asleep soundly by noon. My husband lay down and closed his eyes, and I found the crook of his arm that used to be familiar and made myself a home there. I inhaled slowly, remembered his smell, and knew then that nothing had really changed.

"I'm sorry for what I said," I told him, and he said he was sorry, too.

And for three rainy, afternoon hours, we lay skin to skin, waking every so often to get closer after drifting apart in slumber, always finding each other once more, lacing fingers, tracing constellations of freckle and scar.

They told me that having a child would make me fall more deeply in love with my husband. For the first twelve days, I called them all liars. But on day thirteen, I understood. It was like falling in love a second time. Climbing over mountains and scraping your knees but continuing to climb, tumbling together, deeper and deeper still.

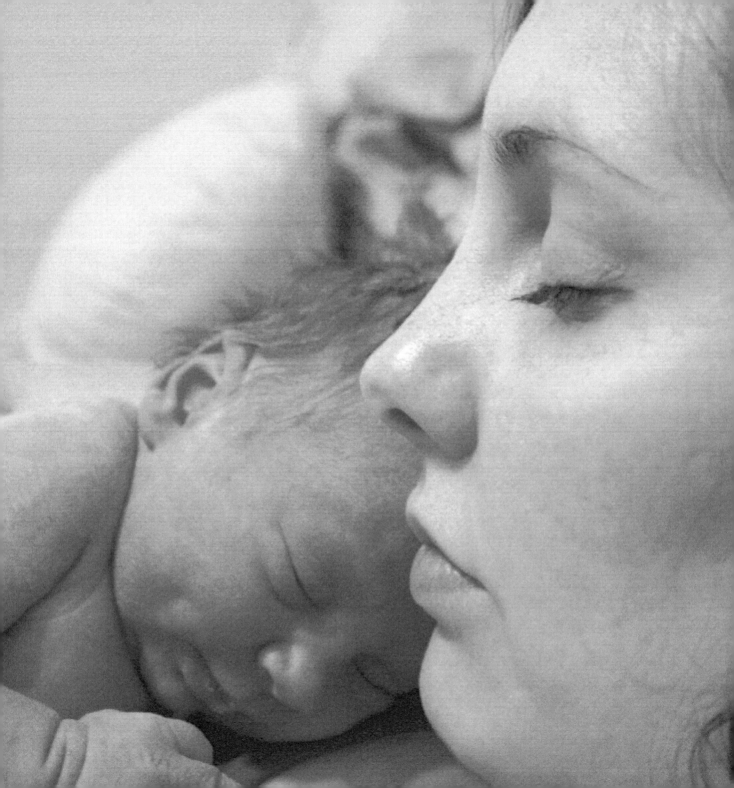

I'm a daughter of a home birth midwife and a birth doula in training. So it probably doesn't come as too much of a surprise when I say that I always dreamed of having a home birth. Although our little Nora June came three weeks early, we had an incredibly dreamy, peaceful, empowering home birth. Now, I say that just so you understand how I entered into my postpartum time - feeling so confident in my body, like I could take on the world.

Right away we started having latch issues, which lead to traumatized nipples, and a milk supply that even at day 9, hadn't seemed to make a full appearance. I felt so low. This is my baby, and I don't even have what it takes to sustain her. I was so discouraged and thought, *how can my body rock labor like that and then the next moment fail my daughter in such a critical way.* She lost 12% of her birth weight and I felt so hopeless. Thankfully, I had some dear momma friends that donated countless ounces of their own breast milk to help sustain my daughter until I could provide for her on my own. Even the generosity of breast milk from other mamas seemed to taunt me though. I cried so many hot tears thinking of all the other women my daughter was being nourished by other than me. It pains me to write that, because I know and believe with everything in me that it takes a village, but in those sleepless days and nights it felt impossible to step outside myself and truly hear that. I remember even saying to my husband, "I love her so much, but I truly don't believe that I have what it takes to be her mama." And I even muttered words about adoption. He was so gentle with me and spoke words of strength that sustained me. After countless breastfeeding support group meetings, lactation consultant sessions we found out that our daughter Nora had both a lip and posterior tongue-tie, which had been part of the reason for the excruciating pain every time we nursed. A naturopath also found out that I had been suffering from mononucleosis, which was another reason for my sad milk supply. I must tell you though, that now, 7 months later, we have a thriving breastfeeding relationship and although I don't have a freezer full of extra milk, my body provides just enough milk for her everyday. And I am grateful. And though you may not believe me now, the fog will rise. You are doing the hardest, most beautiful work. You are brave. You are not alone. You are the perfect mama for your little one. And grace, grace and more grace over you, new mama, for the mother inside of you was just born, too.

It took seven years of dating before we were married. Two years after that, we created a beating heart deliberately hewn from our love. We had knitted ourselves together, one lopsided square after another until we could anticipate one another's movements even when heavy with sleep. I felt the shift coming long before our perfectly pink daughter arrived at home in the cattle-trough-turned-birthing-pool that somehow captured the animal-like efficiency of birth so accurately. It was there, looming in the way my swollen belly cast him aside as I sat so hot, sweaty, and fragile, silently willing him to offer me one more back rub or another cold glass of water. As if being able to read my mind could confirm we would make it through this unchanged.

But, of course he couldn't, and we didn't.

That first night with our tiny orgami-like package resting between us was the loneliest of my life. She was finally here, nine years, nine months in the making, looking just like his recently deceased mother, and my heart wanted to explode in a disarming show of brilliant fireworks. As I watched her tiny chest rise and fall in the darkness he slept soundly, oblivious, always oblivious, to the shift that had occurred. But I saw it clearly; a gulf that felt like miles or years. It was the first time I had ever known him at a distance. In those first hazy days as we danced a love song for our tiny child, I felt almost destroyed by the weight of it all. The overwhelming love for our daughter laced with the heavy burden that that same love implies. And the way I would only see him, now and then, way out there drifting beside me in the same sea, but most definitely not sharing a boat.

The nights that had once seen us intertwined in a warm puppy pile—free to laugh and talk, and sex at will—were replaced by blurry eyes, and sharp elbows to the ribcage as we navigated a landscape filled with endless rocking and angry screaming limbs. In those early days, the dance was ecstatic and crazed and I wondered if I would ever know him again.

you are so much
stronger than
you ever knew.

I am lucky enough to have a village. I have a mother who doesn't wait for me to ask for help. In the days after the birth, my first, she filled our fridge with food, she held my son and told me to go, soak in a bath. I was high from the birth, soaring when I looked at him, but I was confused when I looked at me. Who was I? I was learning to feed him from my body, I was learning this new body, the breasts full and arms aching. I was learning that my husband and I weren't ever going to be the same. We had bonded ourselves together in a way that a marriage certificate never would.

My body had been cracked in half. I moved so slowly around the house, up the stairs and out of chairs especially. I had been through something hard and I hadn't processed it yet. A few days later, I went up the stairs at a normal human pace and I cheered, my sister cheered with me.

Even with a village, the best village, it's hard. But it had a rhythm, a cozy one. Deep like a drum.

The rhythm was feed, feed, feed, rest.

The first thirty days were a haze of round the clock feedings and diaper changes. They were a fog of kisses and warm quick naps and staring at the beautiful alien body that came out of me. There was crying and frustration and red-rimmed eyes. The whole house sagged without sleep.

I was learning him, this wild thing that came from me. Even though I loved him from the first moment, I didn't recognize him. I had to study his knuckles, the curve of the bones in his hand. I watched the lips at my nipple, and I watched the cheeks pumping like a beating heart. I slept when I could. Sometimes though, instead of sleeping, I just held him, laid with him. Watched him. Felt the tiny skeleton, the pebble bones of his spine. I blinked in the milky hours before daylight, watching his pulse blink in his forehead.

I watch my husband hold him. I discover new things to love, new challenges and strains

164

and inspirations that weren't there before. It is work to grow in the same direction. We find moments to connect again, ways to remember how we were before. We hold each other up.

All this information writes over old memories, and in some ways there's a time wall there, at the birth. You can remember things from before but they are cut off; you will never return. You are so much stronger than you ever knew, and your wellspring of love runs so deep. It's connected down at the root to a deep eternal love, and there's a flowing river there we can always drink from.

I will never be the same. And that's great.

his eyes cast
light when I
can't see
beyond
my grief

"Was it hard for you to understand my disappointment with our birth experience?" I asked my husband last night. Our son is five months old, learning to crawl and growing sandy blonde hair in replacement of the dark silk on his head at birth.

"It was different than how I felt," he said. " I just tried to be there for you and give you your space. It was hard to understand that it wasn't just about our healthy baby for you. There were other factors."

Those other factors, simply put, were that I had spent months envisioning a vaginal, medication-free birth. Like many women, I more than planned and prepared for it - I hoped for it in full confidence that I would experience it. So when my son was born via c-section while I was unconscious on the operating table, I was heartbroken. I missed my son's birth.

On top of the physical pain of a c-section and the hormonal swings of post partum, this heartbreak seemed impossible to manage during those first few weeks. I felt damaged, not completely whole. I often thought my husband didn't understand - couldn't understand. Maybe he can't (though not for lacking of trying), but I'm learning that sometimes, a different perspective is more healing than commiseration.

It's easy to fall into the trap of thinking that I was the only person there, the only one experiencing our son's birth. Because I am the mother, my memory of those days reigns supreme, even as time and my growth as a mother change my interpretation. This isn't true, of course. My husband was there, too, experiencing it and remembering it in his own way. When his experience seems to contradict mine, that's a blessing. His eyes cast light when I can't see beyond my grief.

An excerpt from my journal, 1 week postpartum:

December 1, 2014: When I cried about my C section the past few days, Christopher reminded me that there are many special moments to come in Rory's life that I will get to enjoy. I thought he didn't understand; he didn't recognize how I'd missed an important moment in my own life when I was conked out on the operating room table. This afternoon as I rocked Rory to sleep, I understood he was right. Nothing can ever make up for the experience that I lost, but the sweet, quiet hour I spent rocking my newborn son curled up on my chest was no less a precious experience. I can't let what I missed weigh me down with such sorrow that I am unable to be present for all the joy Rory brings to my life already. And I can't let dread of potential yet rare health problems distract me from healing now.

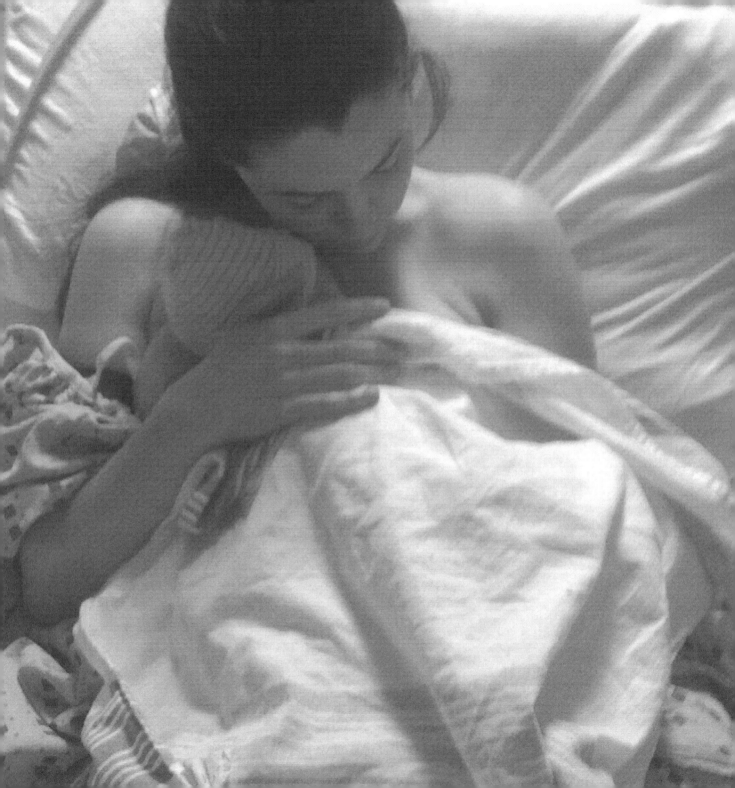

I became pregnant with my sweet Grayson at the end of my twenty-third year. It was the twentieth of June when those double lines appeared. It must have been a warm day; I can still smell the heat. The way a room smells when it's been bathed in the summer sun through an open window. Like fresh grass & honeysuckle. I remember the way the breeze blew the feathers of a dream-catcher that hung from my wall. The shadows of dancing branches at work above me while I lay, perfectly still, on my bedroom floor. On June twentieth of 2013, I met fear. It was the second day in February and I have no idea if my teeth were brushed or if snow was falling outside. But I do know this - on February 2nd of 2014 I was born. A naked, peaceful, heartbreakingly beautiful child lay on my breast. He stared, bravely into my eyes and a magical exchange took place. I am your mom. You are my son. You will always be loved.

Bringing home Grayson was equal parts thrilling and terrifying. It was a lovely concoction of incredible apprehension and an infinite amount of emotion. Mostly, it was unfamiliar. Casey and I were green in experience, unsure of what would come next and frightened by the possibility that we could fail. We didn't. He didn't. I didn't. I did cry, though. And we were exhausted. And on two different occasions Grayson peed on his face, which made me cry again because my God, how could I let my baby pee on his own face? We learned that baby boys will pee everywhere, especially on themselves and most definitely on his nursery walls. We discovered that dishes will sit in the sink, that bed clothes will not always be changed each Sunday, and that being a parent is the most challenging responsibility we will ever face as both individuals and partners. Yet we didn't fail, and I know that's true because I love Grayson every second of every day. In the morning and at night. When I am laughing and crying. In sad and happy moments. I love him with a fire that burns the most hidden parts of my being. Love creeps through my body like a vine up a tree, wrapping around my soul until I think I might burst with joy. It raises me up and grounds me all at once. Deep like the sea and higher than the tallest pine. That is how I love him. That is how I will always love him. When years pass and my hair turns gray and the wind carries sweet melodies across the earth I know I will still hear songs of Grayson and the mother who loved him so. I will hear tales of motherhood and I will laugh and cry and fall to my knees in gratitude for my baby. For this lovely, terrifying adventure. For being Mama.

In the beginning, they're very small and very still, and you might not realize the profound nature of what you've done. But very soon they grow, they reach and pull the glasses from your nose and smile at you when they wake, and suddenly you know that you've created an entire person, and everything you do and everything you've ever said or done will shape them like clay between your palms. This is equal parts terrifying and insanely beautiful.

Last night I sat with KC and said, "They don't tell you how much it hurts to be a mother, or a father. Babies wreck you."

"How do you mean?" He said, leaning against me.

I tried to find the words, but nothing fit properly. "It's like walking around with your skin torn off - everything is so tender and raw. I've never felt so much. You look at this sweet thing, this person, this other-worldly being, and you think, my god, I can't imagine a life before her, or a life without her, and to imagine her hurt or sick or scared makes your entire body ache. She's blown my heart wide open."

He smiled at the floor and nodded. "I agree. You could end a war with this kind of love."

Dear one,

You've reached the end. I'm sure you're feeling full. Take a moment. Take a breath. Unravel all the tight spaces in your heart. Dust off the shame from your shoulders. Rest.

These stories have been picked ripe from our hearts for you. And now that you've tasted them, give them a while to digest. Most mothers are not born in the exact moment that their child joins them earth side. The birth of the mother within takes time, as I'm sure you know. Layers must be removed, peeled back, scraped clean. Bits and pieces of your old self must die, move over, tuck away and make space for the complete and selfless love that will grow like roots in your ribs. Allow it to wash your spirit clean. Nourish yourself with good food, sweet conversation, slow moments, and skin on skin with your velvet babe. This second birth is painful, and lasts longer than the labor preceding childbirth itself. Be gentle with yourself.

With these stories in your pocket, I hope that you feel a little more at home in this new skin you're wearing. I hope that you feel a little less alone. A little more in love. We're here for you. All of us. We have you in our arms, on our shoulders, holding your heart. Softly, with grace.

It takes a village, after all.

Your friend,
Kristen

for you, from us

your story
can heal

your heart.
use the following pages to write it down.

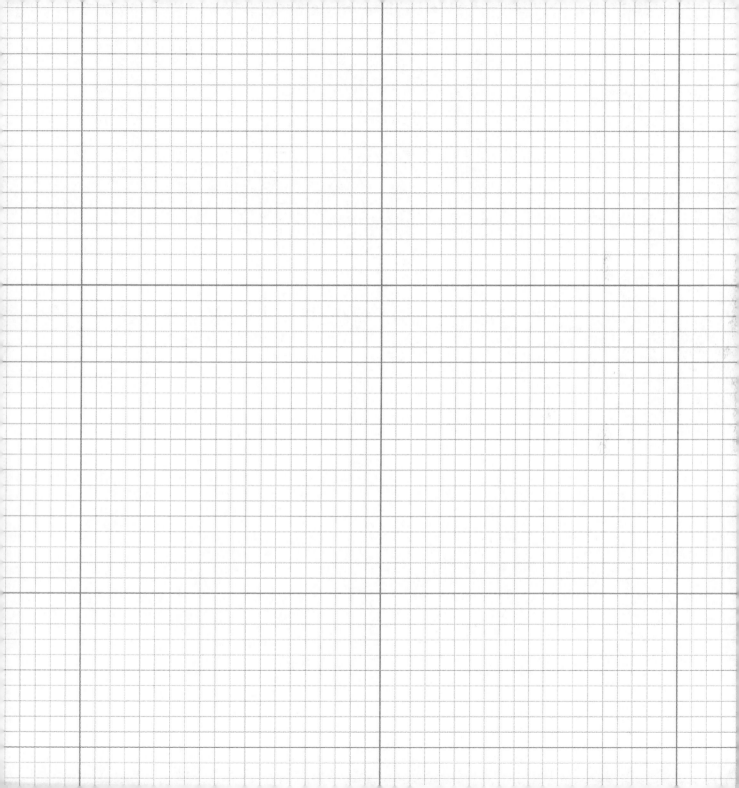

photos accompanying each story used
with permission from the author.

photo accompanying the introduction, as well as pages 104 & 137
were offered by jessica souza. photo on page 4 offered by ashley perlberg.
photo on page 120 offered by gabrielle montgomery.
photo on page 94 offered by amanda bailey.

Made in the USA
San Bernardino, CA
27 May 2015